Conn
Your In
& Everyday
Magic.♥

Dearest Pam ♡

So excited for you to
read this ☺ Thankyou
& welcome to
            Pam-Land ☺

                All my love

Liz Green ♥ ♡ xy

First published in 2016 by Liz Green
Bank Lane, Upper Denby

ISBN: 978-1-911347-03-3

Produced by J R Nicholls Publishing, Denby Dale

Printed and bound in Great Britain by
CPI Group (UK) Ltd, Croydon CR0 4YY

Cover artwork by Corinne Lee-Cooke
www.violetlakestudio.co.uk

Dedication

Thank you to all you fellow life travellers for sharing this journey with me

~

we are all in this together ❤

Foreword ❤

Ever since I was a little girl I have always loved to write, and for years I have had the deep urge to write a book. More recently, I've felt this calling, this magnetic pull, grow stronger and stronger. As you will read in the pages which follow, the magic of synchronicity and Divine Order led me to sharing this with you. Not doing this book was no longer an option – it's my purpose and soul path in life. Have you ever felt like this about something?

What I share in the pages that follow, I do so from my heart to yours, sharing my own life experience and stories as they flow. Simply following the energy without too much of a plan has been a huge learning curve for me, let alone writing my first book by surrendering to the flow and connection of writing, trusting in the possibilities of others resonating with the truths and magic I share. Thank you for being here and sharing this journey with me.

To start with, I wanted to support you to connect with your own truths and inner knowing. This way, you can choose to cherry-pick and go with what feels right to you from that which I share in this book, letting go of anything else.

There are so many personal development books out there, all claiming to tell us what to do to create our dream life - I know I've read heaps of them! Some of them were useful, some weren't, some changed the way I looked at life and some didn't and that's cool. We are all on our own unique individual journeys, we are one of a kind, we are totally YOUnique, as is this Magical YOUniverse.

I will go on to share the magic of life, or everyday magic as I like to call it, and all of its wonderfully wonderful wonders, as well as how to be ok with the not-so-magical times in life, many of which I have experienced first-hand. When I say this, I'm talking about everyday life, the life that we are all living right here, right now. I'm not talking about some jet-set lifestyle, where we all live in mansions and drive sports cars, but simply everyday life as it is and living it in a much more balanced and grounded way by changing our entire outlook on the way life can be and how we feel about it. I'm not saying that all else won't follow if that's the divine plan for you; what I am saying is to let go of any preconceptions, wants and needs and to simply relax into the flow, letting life's tensions go.

I invite you to view this book as a journey that

you are going to take with me, where I will also share magical things which have helped me along the way and you are more than welcome to share in this magic, taking any action you feel inspired to take. It's all good. I will also share my own examples of how I take a different look on life and how I am ok with whatever is happening, providing examples of how you can feel better, regardless of what is happening in your life.

My experiences are shared in layers in this book - stories of past experiences in the UK, what then unfolded as I continued to write the book in Spain, as well as what started to unravel as I returned home, to start the huge task of typing this book up. It's not all pretty, flowery and fluffy, although some of it is; how could it not be? We are talking about magic!

I am very much looking forward to sharing this with you. I really do hope you enjoy reading this as much as I enjoyed writing it and typing it and I am beaming big hugs and lotsa love to you. Thank you for being here on this magical journey and for all of your support.

I hope that in some way, I can support you too.

With love & appreciation, Liz ❤

Introduction ❤

Truth/truːθ/
noun
The quality or state of being true. A belief that is accepted as true.

Believe/bɪˈliːv/
verb
Accept that (something) is true, even without proof.

Magic/madʒɪk/
noun
The power of influencing events by using mysterious or supernatural forces.

What we believe creates our reality around us.

What you believe to be true for you will most probably become your reality. Until now, this is simply a world you have created from the inside out - a world we have created together both consciously and unconsciously. I am inviting you to take a fresh approach to how your YOUniverse is created (btw, as you have already noticed, I like to create new words). It's ok not to follow what already exists and to create something new.

Your YOUniverse can be ahhhhmazing when you start to connect with your inner truth and believe that magical living is possible. Re-connecting and plugging in to the divine Universal Energy that is all around us each and every moment of each and every day. Sometimes, we just forget this and cut ourselves off. It's part of our human 'beingness,' with our often limited patterns, thoughts and behavior's.

Bless us ♥

Life can be tough at times and we all go through a lot of shit - that's the truth. This can no longer be ignored and stuffed down or it will pop up in other places and keep manifesting itself in our lives. Throughout this book, I will support you to connect with that which is ready to clear and to reconnect to who you really are and to your light within. We will take this journey together, going through the ups and downs, the round and arounds and the rollercoaster of life, to hopefully reconnect with your lightness and brightness, which is always within you. Just like the sun behind the clouds or the rainbow on a stormy day, the truth will always shine through.

It is the knowing we have deep within us. Call it instinct, vibes, feelings, hunches, intuition, knowing; maybe even God, Great Spirit, Angels or Universal Power - that's us too! We are the light. We are the creators and co-creators. I'm not saying we are it all as a whole, for me, my truth says we are part of it all. Part of the oneness within this magnificent Universe, we can meld and change how things happen.

Connect with your own YOUniqueness (yes, another one of those words!) Connect with your own YOUnique truth and magical ways and let go of anything which doesn't feel right to you. Trust in those feelings that come from within.

The truth and natural everyday magic of life feels connected, tuned in, turned on and tapped into something far greater than just us in our human form. Trust this - only you know what the infinite possibilities are! Remember, no one else can tell you; they can only advise, as can I.

So, I guess this is my get-out clause. You can read this book and it may change your whole outlook on life, as well as the world around you, or it may not - the last bit is up to you. Connect with your inner truth, believe that anything is possible and believe in the magic of everyday life. This is just the beginning and I'm sooooo excited to be sharing this with you!

Chapter 1

Connecting with your Own Truth ♥

Have you ever had one of those moments in life when someone tells you something is the truth and you feel something's off? Maybe they are telling you to act a certain way or follow a particular path in life. Maybe they are sharing something about themselves, or something they have done, telling you that you should do it too, but it feels wrong to you in some way. You can't explain what doesn't feel quite right about it, but your body's reaction tells you so. You may feel a tightening in your stomach around your solar plexus, which is the area around and above your belly button. You may feel tightness or tension somewhere in your body, maybe around your shoulders, jaw or face. When this happens, our bodies are letting us know what is true for us from within. You may even have a feeling of putting on a 'smile' mask, particularly if you are a people-pleaser, and don't be ashamed to admit this; I know I have been there too and sometimes still try to do this.

You listen, nod, ummm and ahhh in all the right places and smile on the outside, whilst on the inside, you feel those knots of untruth getting tighter and tighter. Congratulations at this point if you are the type of person who speaks up and shares your own truths; keep moving in that direction, as long as it's considerate to others and for the greater good. This is an important one to keep in mind and heart when truth-telling.

The same also goes for truth-telling to ourselves with regard to what we have and what we are creating in our lives. Are you doing that which is true to you? The life you live, the things you do, the actions you take?

We are all doing what we think is our best, flowing through these different life-levels of realisation, waking up and evolving as we go. All in good time for each and every one of us, be gentle on yourself, whatever stage you are at. This is a time of great change and powerful shifts and when shift happens, sometimes shit happens too!! This is a transitional period - no need to jump off the cliff without the wings to fly and fear hitting the decks. It can be a steady, magical journey, giving us the chance to firstly learn how to build our wings before we jump and then, how to put them together and strap them onto our back with perfect, divine timing. Maybe this will be on the way down and that's ok too - just make sure it feels right to you.

It's time to speak up when required; to change and move towards your own truths and to be true to you! When we are true to ourselves and others around us, magical things happen. Remembering to come from a place and space of love and understanding, both with others and with yourself. These feelings that guide us are that of our Inner Spirit and the Spirit that is around us, always there guiding us in the best possible direction. It's up to us whether we listen to this truth or not.

This intuition and our feelings and vibes will always let us know. Everything vibrates, including words, people, places, situations and circumstances. We live in a vibrational world and to powerfully connect with these vibes will transform your life.

How do you feel right now? Are you being true to you?

Are there any areas in your life which feel tight, restrictive and heavy rather than light, open and free flowing?

Connecting with your inner truth and following that each and every day will give you a feeling of expansion and clarity. You will feel like you are wearing your 'Vibrational Angel Wings' and your whole world will start to reflect that. Soon, you will be flying high!

I would love to share an example from my own life of how this works. As a fellow traveler on the journey of life, I have learnt these things along the way. I am sharing from my heart to yours, by way of life examples and how this process of awakening to these truths, changes the world around us.

Seven years ago, I was working in the corporate world as a Senior Account Manager for a large printing company. I started working full time when I was seventeen years old and that was twenty-one years ago. It was drilled into me that I had to get a good job and make a living and that this, in turn, would create a life. I'm sure many of you have been told this 'truth.'

So I came to believe it and, in turn, created it. Remember, what we believe creates our reality around us. I believed the truth at the time was to work really hard to get on in life (oh, it all sounds so wrong when I share this in the here and now). I did just that and started working as a trainee swiftly working my way up that particular snakes and ladders game.

Around the age of thirty, I started to learn more about personal development and in particular, the Law of Attraction. I started to open up to new ways of thinking and being. At the time, it was much more of the head-led stuff, mindset, affirmations and, yes, lots of good vibes too, but my life wasn't really feeling all that good-vibed. In fact, it felt off. I was stressed, tense, uptight and really not connecting with my light. I had created a life which didn't feel like my own, trying to make life work and working really hard at it in the process. I felt like the lead actress playing a role which wasn't really me. Have you ever felt like that?

The more I learnt about the Universe and how Law of Attraction works, the more 'off' what I had created started to feel. Awakening to these untruths eventually started to make me feel worse than I had before I knew about all this stuff. I wished I hadn't taken the blue pill (or is it the red pill?) and opened up a right old can of vibrational worms. I had more knowledge, and at the time what I had learnt felt like truth to me, not much else did. The worms were well and truly out and squirming all over the place and so was I!

So, I decided to take big action steps towards living a more inspired life and connecting more with what I was feeling. I took these big action steps believing that when we take inspired action, we see t h e Law of Attraction in action. The problem was, looking back, it wasn't all as inspired as I first thought.

My belief system at the time, and I still know this to be true, is that when we are inspired, we are in~spirit, and when we are in~spirit, we are connecting to our inner truth; our Divine Spirit within.

For me, at that time, it meant joining a community of like-minded people who were creating businesses using the Law of Attraction and lots of people who were using 'not-so-always-inspired action' and sharing this with people all over the world. At the time, I didn't realise that it was a network marketing company, selling spiritual community-based, self-empowerment trips. Some of the people involved were much more interested in making money than sharing in the community spirit. For me, it felt a lot like a non-religious faith of the Law of Attraction. My work colleagues at the printing company thought I had finally lost the plot and joined a cult, and maybe in some ways, I had!

I now recognise that being raised as a Jehovah's Witness (often called 'The Truth') had deeply ingrained into me that these kind of communities are a good thing and I'm not saying they aren't - that's for you to decide. The problem I had was I was turning my other cheek to the parts of it which felt 'off' and not listening or connecting with my true feelings which were coming up about it all. I re-mortgaged the house got loans and credit cards and invested tens of thousands of pounds based upon what others within the community told me I could believe. It didn't stop there. I went for it big time by jumping off the cliff without even knowing how to start to build my wings.

After a 'this is the final straw' week at work, I was so upset that my chap said he would sell his sports car to give me a little money to be able to leave and 'try' and 'make' things work, with 'try' and 'make' being the operative words! It's ironic, because all of the material things we had focused on manifesting when we first learnt about the Law of Attraction were now starting to leave our lives. My feelings about this whole situation were too important to ignore. I could no longer spend the majority of my week living a life which felt like a lie to whom I really was. The following morning, I quit my job, handed back the keys to the company car, told them I was going to do yoga and find myself and I left, leaving behind the big wage packet too!

A part of me genuinely believed that the Universe would provide for me financially and that this business would work if I took such a big leap of faith. I was visualising cheques coming and money flowing in, as if they were going to start pouring out of the light sockets and the tap every time I turned them on! Obviously, this is not what happened and it was a very different story, as you will discover as you continue reading. Without me realising it, it was as if I was stripping back to basics and being guided to simplify.

Lots of tears of happiness and most probably denied tears flowed freely as I embarked on my new and shiny life in 'Liz~Land'... or so I thought! I still wasn't fully connecting with my truth and it became clear I'd replaced the corporate world with another similar company which was overseeing what I was doing and how I was 'performing', they were also being dishonest and out of integrity. Looking back on this makes me feel totally 'out-of-integrity' with the person I am today. That said, I believe integrity means 'to integrate it all.' This new path I had jumped onto gave me lots and lots of opportunities to start the process of integration, reconnecting and realigning with where I was meant to be at the time. I kept receiving more and more signs and an inner knowing that something was off; I was becoming more and more fearful and also worrying about money due to my heavy investment. Part of me was hanging on for dear life - or should that be fear life!

Looking back, I totally get that it was meant to be, and in some ways, it was the truth for me back then. By going through this process over the course of around three years, immense and sometimes intense truth bubbled to the surface, supporting me to cleanse and clear my vibes and to totally transform the world around me. I was becoming more of me by starting to identify what felt right and what felt wrong. More about that later on, but for now, I will say that it formed a fabulous belief system for me...

I believe that when we connect with what we don't want, don't like and don't resonate with in life, including people, places, circumstances and situations, then we can reconnect with that which we do want, like or even love. If we didn't taste the foods we don't like, how would we know the foods we do like?

When we go through this kind of contrast we have the opportunity to reconnect with that which does resonate. Just like the tuning forks which ping together with perfect alignment, this kind of alignment feels really good especially when we have experienced misalignment and the tuning forks not pinging together.

We are all so different, which is where the cherry-picking comes in. We get to choose what we pick in life; what we do and do not believe in, and sticking with the cherry analogy, you wouldn't pick the rotten ones, would you? Or if the cherry looked good on the outside but tasted off when you ate it, you wouldn't eat another would you?

I admit I've eaten my fair share of rotten vibrational cherries in my time, and sometimes still do. That's how life and our human experience can be. The difference is, I now know when I am doing it and swiftly move in the direction of better-tasting stuff, which aligns with my truth and where I am on my journey. I also do my best to still love, accept and appreciate myself, no matter what choices I make. Do you still love, accept and appreciate yourself regardless of what choices you have made or what proverbial cherries you have picked?

Being these things called Human Beings (not human doings btw) can be a rollercoaster of a journey, with the ups and downs, the round and arounds, the ins and outs, the knowing, the not knowing, the wins, the losses, the ease, the dis...ease. This whole job lot is what life is and this is what we are here to live in, with all its depth and richness of experience and if we are to accept and be ok with what has come before us, what lies ahead of us and relaxing into each 'now' moment as much as we can and being as ok with it as we can, then to me, this feels like truth.

What do you feel? What's your truth about the rollercoaster of life?

Is that serving you well?

Chapter 2

Breathing in Life & Clearing your Vibes ❤

During this chapter, I am going to ask you to play along with me - and sorry if you are reading this on the train, bus, plane or in a public place, as we are going to get a little physical. This is the perfect time for me to be sharing this, as I am about to have a lovely massage on the beach in about half an hour. Yes, I know that sounds clichéd that I'm writing my book on the beach. I don't live here in Almunecar in Spain, it's just that the Universe sent me a perfectly synchronistic opportunity to be here in this space and place to dedicate myself to writing. Some would say I am living the dream here on the beach; for me, I am living my dream at home, in the countryside. At Greenwood cottage with my chap and my furry babies, Levi and Lloyd the cats and Magical Milo my big black doodly Labradoodle. Whilst at home, a lot of my days are spent out in nature doing lots of lovely dog walks, as well as sharing my intuitive energy coaching and getting creative by making jewellery, plus lots of other day-to-day living-life kind of stuff. This means that where I find myself today, here on the beach in Spain, gives me the perfect opportunity to write as I have lots of free time on my hands.

I also have to add I've just looked over to my left to see a T-Shirt saying 'GENIUS,' which I feel is a fantastic 'sign' to say I'm totally supported being here sharing this. The synchronicity of the Universe sending the word 'genius' to me and to that part of me who wonders if I really am, or even can be, a writer. Well, I guess I am, because here I am sharing my genius! I am clearing that part of me who doesn't believe I can be and let's clear and clean that part of you who says you can't be a genius too! We are all geniuses in our own YOUnique way and we all have genius gifts to share with the world.

Anyway, I digress. More about the magic of synchronicity later - it's my favourite truth: the magic of synchro's. Anyway, back to the physical stuff! I know I'm keeping you intrigued... not long now.

I was going to ask you to close your eyes, but then you won't be able to read the words which follow and that wouldn't be a very genius thing to do now, would it? So for now, simply breathe nice and deeply and relax as much as you can. Once you know how to do this, you can do it with your eyes closed if you prefer.

Do you feel that you are breathing right for your body? Tune into it and notice how you are breathing as you continue to read on. I read lots and lots of books and a few years back, I realised when I was reading (or writing for that matter), I was holding my breath or shallow breathing.

So, please keep breathing deeply and fully, as we take more information in when we breathe correctly in this way. In and out, ahhhhhhh... In through the nose and out through the mouth. Ahhhhhhhhhhh...

I believe we should introduce yoga and correct breathing techniques into schools and be taught this at as early an age as possible. I mean, come on, it's what keeps us alive, healthy and well! Yes, our bodies breathe naturally, particularly when we are asleep or resting, but a lot of the time during waking hours, we may not be achieving our full breathing potential and withholding breath when we are connecting with those pesky non-truths I talked about in the last chapter.

The best way I feel I can share this, to help you breathe more deeply is to imagine yourself as an opera singer. When we breathe in, our bellies should expand and fill with air, expanding our bodies as the air moves from the stomach up to the chest and shoulders, raising us up and uplifting us as we breathe in the oxygen. Yoga classes helped me to connect with this as well as a process called Breathwork and Rebirthing, which I experienced in Peru and continued to do upon my return home. More about Peru later!

For now, breathing. Deeply.   Relaxed.

Breathe in through the nose and out through the mouth. On your in breath, expand. On your out-breath, let go; belly softening and shoulders relaxing. Here comes the fun bit (or should that be funny bit)!

Start to wiggle your shoulders round and around and up and down. Wiggle wiggle.

Keep going with this movement. We are loosening up, allowing the energies to flow and anything which is stuck to become unstuck.

Now, move your arms. Open them wide and stretch whist you keep wiggling (I did say sorry if you are reading this in public - lighten up and have fun with it!). Lift your arms up and then wide, stretch it all out. Open up and expand!

Now, along with this, start to wiggle your jaw, round and around, side to side and open wide. Say ahhhhhhhhhhhh. Massage around your ears with your fingers, rubbing around the front and back. Get loose and loosen this energy up, loosey goosey!

Do you hear cracking noises? It's ok, so do I. Yes I'm doing this with you too! This is releasing the tensions we hold, often around our shoulders, jaw and ears. Keep wiggling and moving and as the cracking disappears and your shoulders, jaw and face become softer, you will start to feel a sense of openness. Your ears feel clearer and shoulders feels softer. This is the feeling of expansion. Your body may also make you feel like yawning, which is good for taking in extra oxygen and relaxing. Keep breathing deeply, open up, yawn and stretch – it's all good! When we breathe out, we are naturally clearing our vibes and letting go of toxins, in turn taking in the good stuff.

When I go to yoga classes, I call it 'Yawning Yoga,' because I yawn all the way through, letting go of my tensions (and I know I am an intense person) and having this way of letting go serves me well, as does this exercise. I recommend doing it daily, especially in the evening, to clear any blocks you may have been holding onto from the daytime. Do what feels good for you.

Breathe...**R**elax...**A**llow. Aka   B R A

Please be sure to use your BRA every day, and yes, that goes for the blokes too! Maybe this is why the magical word is **abra**cada**bra**?

This will give you magical powers! Especially when dealing with life's more difficult circumstances. Why do you think mothers-to-be are taught breathing exercises?

Breathe...**R**elax...**A**llow.   LET GO...

How are you feeling?

Open your arms up wide as you continue fully 'belly-breathing' (or at least one of your arms if you are holding this book in the other - lol!); look up to the heavens and appreciate where you are right here, right now. The supply of oxygen from nature is infinite and we are sooooo abundant! How cool is that?

Breathe, let go, breathe, let go
and E X P A N D your energy.

In this space, the truth flows from within. These feelings of expansion are light and bright. Can you feel this truth?

To absolutely know this truth, it's good to experience the opposite of this. The polarity at the other end of the scale.

Let's do some more movement, but this time in the opposite direction, the polarity. Bring your arms close to your body and grasp your fists tightly, whilst at the same time tightening your shoulders and your face, holding your breath for a few moments and tightly contracting. Feel the contrast of this to the previous exercise - the contraction and tightness.

Now, B R E A T H E, let go...

Open your fists and relax your shoulders. Take another breath and wiggle your shoulders, jaw and face. Do what you did before and loosen back up, opening your arms widely and breathing deeply. Now, pop your BRA back on!

Contraction is the opposite of expansion and when we feel this contraction - this dense, dark, tense and heavy feeling, we are out of our natural flow. Whenever we feel this way, it is the most important time for us to let go, open up, breathe and feel the inspiration. Inspiration comes from the word inspire, the word inspire originates from the Latin word *Inspirare,* which, in its literal sense, means 'the act of inhaling.' When we are breathing in life, we are inspired, I also believe being inspired means we are in~spirit. How wonderful is that?

I am certain that this feeling of expansion, of being inspired or in~spirit, connects us with our truths, whereas contraction connects us with the opposite of this. I believe that when something feels open and light, this shows us our own truth from within and our opposite feelings show us our own non-truths and that which doesn't resonate from within. We are meant to live as expanded and connected beings, literally breathing in life's energy.

Think about your life, where you are and who you are in the now. Connect with what you do in life for a living and then with what you would love to be doing. Do you feel expansion or contraction? Think about your emotions and feelings, tuning in to something you feel worried or fearful about. How does that feel? Does it feel true to you? Remember the contraction is letting you know it's untrue, maybe it's telling you there is nothing to be worried or fearful about and you can now relax and expand into lighter feelings. Now, tune into something you feel love and happiness for or something you are excited about. How does that feel? Do you feel the lightness and brightness?

Can you take inspired action and change things in your life so you feel more expansion? There is no rush - we are in a transitional period. It's all good!

I would love to share with you how breathing deeply, clearing my vibes and using my vibrational BRA has helped and supported me (btw, I am talking about a vibrational BRA as well as a real one – no-one wants saggy boobs now do they? lol!).

Not long after I left the corporate world and just a month after a trip away with the community I now found myself a part of, I was diagnosed with Meniere's Dis...ease. I believe dis...ease is our body's way of saying it's not at ease, it's uneasy, tense and stressed in some way. This particular dis...ease that manifested in my life was all about balance and it appears in the form of severe vertigo attacks (I prefer to call them 'episodes' to soften this). Meniere's also includes dizziness, deafness and feelings of disconnection.

At that time, I had just returned from Mexico, where I had taken part in my very first Firewalk and lots of big changes and vibrational shifts were happening. I was awakening to new life -levels and what was really possible in life. My chap and me also did an arrow break and rebar bend, where we broke arrows against our neck and bent a rusty old metal scaffolding bar using only our necks whilst walking towards each other - it simply melted like butter and bent in half. This is the power of self-belief and trusting that anything is possible when you believe it to be so. I knew I was on the right track by opening up to this, but a part of me kept holding on to the old ways of being.

Trying, needing and wanting to make things work, taking lots and lots of action and maybe not always the inspired kind. After the Firewalk, I knew in my heart that I was powerful beyond any measure I had previously thought, as we all are, and yes that goes for YOU too! When we have the belief and the faith, then anything IS possible.

Impossible = I'm~Possible.

Can you feel the truth in that?

Maybe a part of you is saying no, which is only natural as it's ingrained into us to believe it when we see it, rather than believe it first to then see it or experience it.

Here's a nice little tester for you to connect with who you really are and who and what you can be.

'Feel' into the following two statements and imagine me saying these to your face and REALLY meaning them or should that be MEAN~ing them.

Statement One:

YOU ARE A TOTALLY RUBBISH, NO GOOD, USELESS, LIMITED BEING. YOUR HOPES AND DREAMS ARE A TOTAL WASTE OF TIME BECAUSE YOU WILL NEVER AMOUNT TO ANYTHING. IF I WERE YOU, I WOULDN'T EVEN BOTHER GETTING OUT OF BED IN THE MORNING!!!

Feel good?

Any feelings of tightness and contraction

there?

A little side note here: If any part of you feels like that is true in any way, or maybe you even speak about yourself like that, then how's that serving you? But more importantly, how does it FEEL? Remember the truth feels light and bright and I certainly didn't feel that lightness and brightness even typing the words above, let alone saying them to you!

Now 'feel' into statement two:

YOU ARE A BEAUTIFUL, EXPANSIVE, LIGHT BEING FILLED WITH INFINITE POSSIBILITES. YOUR HOPES AND DREAMS ARE MAGICAL AND YOU CAN BE, DO AND HAVE ANYTHING YOU DESIRE. YOU ARE TOTALLY AHHHHMAZING! YOU ARE A GIFT TO THE WORLD!

Feel good?

Can you feel the expansion and lightness in this?

And for any part of you that is disbelieving

this, are you open to clearing that with forgiveness and love for these limited thoughts you may have been believing?

Feel into your own truths and tune into where they are coming from and what thoughts about yourself they are based upon. Let's clear the way for all of us to be more and more of statement number two. Can you imagine a world filled with these versions of us? How cool would that be?

We are all infinite light filled beings and we CAN do anything, even though we sometimes don't believe it. Remember that what we believe ultimately creates our worlds around us.

If I can walk across hot coals, break arrows and bend rusty old rebars with my neck, then so can you. And you don't have to do it to believe you are that powerful - just know this to be true. I will say it again, if I can do it so can you!

Back to my story about the dis...ease which had manifested itself in my life and how, on the one hand, being at such a life transforming event made me feel like a superhero, but on the other hand, I was filled with worries and fears about what my world in 'Liz~Land' would become. Until that point, I had only ever really known work and working hard at life. The worries and fears had me holding my breath a lot and it was almost as if I had to hold myself up because I felt so insecure about life and wasn't sure how I would support myself. So I decided to push the feelings down and get really, really busy with it. I was 'trying' to sell the personal development excursions alongside the community of other people all trying to do the same, with very few succeeding in anything at all. I had a little success, but only enough to recover what I had invested, and by this point, I needed the money to live off - 'need' being the operative word. This felt like a very needy time in my life.

I decided to turn it around, doing what I did best, which was to share my journey with others and YouTube gave me an amazing and free way to do this. My chap had the inspired idea of calling myself Liz Green, Law of Attraction Queen, and he created a fabulous cartoon picture of me with a crown on. I think he did it as a joke to start with, but I loved the quirkiness of it, which reflected the 'me at the time' really well. I was blogging and making lots and lots of videos to share with lovely people like you, about the magic of life and how wonderful it can be, which it can, in a much more balanced and grounded way.

During this period, I was very one-sided, focusing solely on the good vibes and blocking out everything else, including some of my own truths which were trying to surface. They wanted to let me know I was going in the right direction, but maybe not always on the right path or in the right flow. I was paddling upstream a lot of the time, rather than allowing the waters of life to carry me in the best possible direction. I was basically pushing noodles up a hill!

Have you ever felt that way?

That said, I do believe that we are always right where we are meant to be in life at each and every moment. Each path we walk along holds lessons for us to learn and clarity to be connected with from the not-so-good feeling contrasty stuff. If we never tasted the sour, how would we know what sweet tasted like?

I was intensely focused on going for it full-on with a 'no matter what' attitude, which meant that I was sometimes ignoring my body's truths at the time. I was trying to push down feelings and emotions or stuff down the feelings which weren't of a high vibration; blocking stuff out and in many ways, blocking out life and its rich tapestry of the reality we create for ourselves.

Basically, I was saying "talk to the hand cause the ears ain't listening," at which point, I started to go deaf. The Universe was answering that which I was vibrating, and that which I was vibrating, I was creating. I didn't want to hear the shitty stuff and there were certain truths I wasn't connecting with or hearing. I was filtering, ignoring, reframing, saying "that's not a match" and turning the other cheek. Actually, it was all a perfect match. It always is. What we vibrate, we create. There's absolutely no point in turning away, or even running away from the things we are manifesting in life. More will come until we feel it, heal it and clear up our vibes on it and then we can start to morph and change the world around us.

At this time, I also started to feel really dizzy, ungrounded and off-balance, which was a perfect match, reflecting how I was being. All give, give, give and do, do, do, with not much 'me' time or time for chilling and certainly no time to recharge my batteries. I was running on empty. Looking back, I really enjoyed this time and learnt so much. It's like the old saying about not changing a thing about the past, as it made us who we are today and I feel that is so true and absolutely spot-on. Maybe I am just saying that to make myself feel better, just like we say it's lucky when a bird shits on your head! Coping mechanisms - It's all good!

Around this time, I also started doing an online show called *The Pioneers of Positive Change* and manifested connecting with some wonderful spiritual teachers and guides, or as some would say, GURUS.

Look at the letters in GURU ~ G U R U ~ Gee You Are You. We are each our own guru and have all the answers within (when we tune in, that is).

So yes, I feel what was happening in my life at that time was all totally meant to be. I was also reading lots and lots of books and listening to lots and lots of videos online. I was literally swamping myself with Law of Attraction related stuff and all manner of techniques and methods.

I was in a spin and so was my body.

It was at a Law of Attraction manifesting event, which I had helped to plan and orchestrate in London over the previous six months or so, when I had my worst ever Meniere's 'attack' or 'episode.' I was absolutely gutted, as I had just got down from the stage after introducing the day ahead and 'BAM!' I had to be rescued and 'chill' back to balance. I could probably write a full chapter on what happened that day, but I will keep it short and not-so-sweet. There was humour involved when I look back on it now, but at the time, I felt terrified and I was miles away from home with only a couple of friends there who knew only a tiny bit about this condition, along with a room full of people who thought I lived an ideal life as Liz Green, Law of Attraction Queen! Oh my! What an embarrassing situation to be in. I just felt like a total failure, and, in some ways, a fraud, because I hadn't been totally honest with people about my 'negative' manifesting and had only really been sharing all of the 'positive' magic, just briefly touching on the dis...ease, saying that I would magically manifest it away and heal myself. I simply wasn't going there and wasn't being true to the situation, always trying to reach for hope with an underlying current of fear and worry.

I know now that it's all magic; all of our feelings and emotions and everything that we manifest in life. We just choose to label it with the words negative or positive, good or bad, light or dark. Balance is allowing it all to be as it is; as life is.

Having the need to puke into an antique crystal vase worth £3000, at that time, just did not feel like fun, or magic for that matter, and that was coupled with not being able to see or hear properly, nor to explain what was happening. When my friend finally managed to get us a taxi, the driver was refusing to take me back to the hotel, because he thought I was blind drunk. We sorted it eventually, but it really wasn't good at the time. I just kept remembering that I needed to breathe, but my body felt so tense.

It's really symbolic regarding when and how this all happened and it definitely gave me a HUGE wake-up call; a 'Universal Bitch Slap' so to speak. Nowadays, I know that I don't need these kinds of slaps around the face and I can tune in to my truth of what my body wants in each moment, rather than it having to be such a harsh realisation. Although at the time, if I am being really honest with you, it took me a while to listen to my body. When I returned from London, I got right back on the horse, doing seminars and workshops, talks and meet-ups. There I was once again, getting busy with it!

However, during that time, I did start to wake-up to what felt like my truth about vibe clearing and letting stuff come up and out. Until I got ill, I was holding stuff in; stopping, blocking or ignoring the deeper levels of my emotions. Emotion means energy in motion and the emotions have to flow and be in motion, and that goes for all emotions, even the ones we may have been taught to ignore or hide away. If the emotions are not energy in motion, or if blockages are occurring, they will manifest in other ways in order to release. For me, this was via a dis...ease, which clearly showed me that I was off-balance and which had me projectile vomiting all over the place, as well as the other not-so-nice bodily functions which come along with this! My body was purging in every way it could, including the tears of frustration, sadness, guilt, self- judgement, failure, fear, worry, and the list goes on...

I am being called to introduce another layer to my book - not on the phone or by my spirit (lol!), but called by the truth from within me, and maybe that's what the ringing is in my ears! I hope that it disappears when I share this with you, as something's connecting all of this.

The layer I want to add is that I am back at home now, typing up the words that I wrote in Spain last week. I am sat in the garden in the chilly sunshine and the mother hen from next door has popped over the wall to visit me, as I take a break and have a drink of my 'breathe deep' tea in my favourite rainbow mug, which has the message 'be proud of who you are' on it. Tears are welling up inside of me as I type this here today, as, since yoga class yesterday evening, I've been feeling rather off-balance. Yoga was so aligned with what I'd been typing here in this chapter before I left - it was all about breathing and balance. I was up in the night feeling very dizzy and disconnected and the feelings continued into today. I would describe the feeling as 'wonky.'

I've had lots of tears to release about this, as I know this helps to clear me. If I hold them in, I get tighter and tenser and I begin to feel dizzier. I know, Dizzy Lizzy! It's ironic, as I used to get called that as a kid... No coincidences here!

A coincidence = an incidence that coincides. Meant to be.

I feel that by almost reliving this time in my life and by sharing the stories, then the 'me-in-the now' is starting to match up with that vibration again, so my body starts to resonate with it. Then, in comes the part of me which is still scared to go there with the feelings bit, in case I attract even more crap stuff, so I am feeling into this and knowing that all is well; it's all in Divine Order and if I am supposed to feel this way again whilst sharing this with you, that's ok too. I am going to breathe, relax and allow.

I am going to put into practice what I preach, feel it to heal it and be ok with whatever's coming up.

On a side note, I also know that I am meant to be writing about Meniere's dis...ease and sharing that which helped me at the time. I started a blog called *'Create Balance ~ Find Hope'* around three or four years ago and I haven't been there or revisited it recently. "Ok Magical

Universe, I will go there, but this time around, you don't need to slap me, as I'm tuning in!" I also plan to write my second book on this very subject and think it will be called *'Mastering Menieres the Magical Way'.*

Anyway, I digress, now back to the story (and that's what it is - it's all a story!)... This particular dis...ease made me really, really ill. It was like someone had thrown me out of an airplane with no parachute, which was so similar to the feelings I had when I left work. In between sleeping and puking, I would drink lots and lots of water and breathe as deeply as I could (water is filled with oxygen too, so helps to calm in the same way as breathing does).

When I was in the midst of 'episodes,' I would pray to the Universe, the Angels, God Source Energy and Great Spirit, to help me to clear whatever was bringing all of this about. During these times, the more deeply I could let go, relax, and, most importantly, breathe and the more relaxed my shoulders, jaw and face were, the easier these episodes cleared and passed. The tenser I became, the worse it became.

Like I mentioned before, I used to cry a lot too. The tears would flow freely. Sometimes, my chap would say "don't cry, you will make it worse;" a saying many of us heard as kids. I always replied with "it feels worse to hold the tears in. I have to let it flow." During these times, I would make sure I had something with a love heart to focus on, laser-focused on the love and forgiveness for what was happening and what was coming up.

This was such a valuable lesson in life. I feel I have cleared a lot of it and I have been fully back in balance for the last two years, apart from a few echoes, like today. When these echoes come, I am very sensitive to them and tune in right away. Sometimes, it's because on a practical level, I've been doing too much, or on a vibrational level, I've been worrying. Sometimes, when I am slipping back into my old ways of the answers and spiritual solutions being outside of me; when I start to look 'out there' instead of within, then I feel off-balance. Like today, for example, there have been a few things going off which are ready to change and I am connecting with this energy - trusting the process.

Fast forwarding here (and I may backtrack again later in the book, in particular about our trip to Peru, because I LOVED IT!), we went to Peru before moving to the countryside where we now live. I took part in a Breathwork and Rebirthing Ceremony. It was the following day that the Chief Daddy, Sharman Don Ramone, who is now free flying in spirit after dying last year, bless his soul, gave me a message during our time in Machu Picchu. Everyone else's message was long and wordily translated and sounded super cool. Mine, on the other hand, was short and sweet – he said "breathe more and relax."

So I did just that, and during the breathwork, I experienced huge spiritual shifts and clarity and I continued my journey with it once I returned from Peru. I have to add here that I no longer do the breath 'work' bit, as no work is required; I guess that at the time, I was still working at life.

After moving to the country, I have experienced a few more episodes with the dis...ease, which I feel are reminders and realignments. They reminded me to relax and to get more grounded, as well as allowing me to have a deeper level of clearing and clarity. I am open to the clearings and clarity coming in a much nicer way from now on.

"Thank you, Magical Universe. I'm listening! And in case this dis...ease comes back into my life, or any others for that matter, then I promise I will listen then too, if that's the way things flow."

What do you feel about any dis...ease in your life and how can you feel better about it? Let go of resistance and align with balance.

With that said, I am feeling this is a good time for a swim in the sea, before moving onto the next chapter, which is going to be all about getting caught up in stuff. Now I've opened up a third 'typing this up at home' layer to the book, I have to say that it feels weird to be saying "I am going for a swim," although I did have a nice warm bath this morning and I am now onto my second cup of tea in the garden. The message on the tea says "Let your heart speak to others hearts." I kept getting this message whilst in Spain last week - fab synchro's!

Btw, my massage on the beach was ahhhhhhhmazing! Totally connected and expansive. I was grateful that I took an extra gratitude bracelet I had made, to give to her and say thank you. Perfection!

Thank you, thank you, thank you ♥

Chapter 3

Getting Caught Up in Stuff ❤

This is going to be a short and sweet, yet very freeing chapter. It's time to be easy about stuff and let go of the vibrational traps we sometimes get caught up in.

We can, as human beings, become easily influenced and swayed as to which directions we should take in life. In the world today, there are so many paths to follow and beliefs to be had - lots of cool stuff and not-so-cool stuff too; all of which we can become influenced by. This includes both religious and spiritual practices, as well as many other ways of being, which are offered. I guess we can be caught up in anything in life; for some this may mean TV programmes or certain places to go and be every day, maybe even places of work or certain clubs to be part of.

Once again, this is a matter of what feels true to you, during all the different stages of life. As we are growing up, from being small children to young adults, this world and those around us can be really influential. This reminds me of a Bible quote I used to be told when I was a kid: "Bad association spoils useful habits." I mentioned earlier that I was raised as a Jehovah's Witness, which had a huge impact on who I am today, as well as the person I have become and, yes, that includes being a rebel! Rebelling from that which I feel may want to keep me trapped in something that differs from my own truth (now I know how to listen to my own truth, that is!) I have to add here, and once again say, I wouldn't change anything about my upbringing. I had a very loving and supportive family environment, which again has helped me become who I am today and I love my parents dearly, they are truly amazing people.

I am also not saying that following a particular way of being or being part of a certain religion or community is wrong. I am a big believer in 'each to their own.' What I will say is this: we should always tune into our own vibes and our own feelings on what the truth is to us, and the great thing is, you know how to do that now from what I shared in the last chapter!

I also want to add here that I don't necessarily feel that "bad associations spoil useful habits," as the useful stuff can stick around and the bad associations or circumstances can give us the clarity to be more of who we really are. The key for me, I feel, is to stay connected and tune in regularly. Also bringing in the balance that if we are hanging around with a certain person or people who are negatively focused, then we must be resonating with this, or have something to clear around this if we choose change.

Like when I was little, my upbringing taught me there was going to be an Armageddon, that the world would end and that all of the bad people would die, so obviously I wanted to be as good as I could be. We were also taught not to hang around with people who weren't part of the religion, because they would be worldly and would cause bad influence, hence a part of me believed that and created it. Not the world ending bit, but the bad-vibed friends bit. As for the world ending, I will share more on that later. It has ended and is ending in a different way; no four horsemen of the apocalypse required this time around thank you very muchly!

At the end of the last chapter, I talked about the dis...ease making me uneasy. At that time, I used lots and lots of techniques, which were fab for each different stage of my journey until that point and I'm sure you have lots of techniques you use to help you feel better (and I'm not talking about the wine or beers here, although, yes, that sometimes helps - or not as the case may be lol). In case you don't have many vibe clearing techniques, or only have the latter 'wine' one, or if you are wondering what they even are, then I will share more on this subject later. Firstly, I feel it's important to identify healthy connections with our belief systems, as well as the polarity of this, the not-so-healthy ones.

I believe that nothing should ever take over us, consume us or possess us and our lives. I don't feel any of us should only have one belief system, especially not for the whole of our lives; to be open feels better. It's good to remember that everything that's 'out there' in the world was created by someone and they also have their own path and their own resonance. If we resonate with them and what they offer at different stages of our lives, then that's cool too and then when we no longer resonate, we let go and move along. Like what I am offering here in this book - you choose what feels right for you.

Cherry-picking! We choose which cherries we pick and when we pick them. Here I am with the cherry-picking examples again and I must say I do love cherries! If we picked too many cherries and ate them all at once, we might get belly ache. I reached the point where I had a spiritual belly ache and once again, the Universe gave me a wake-up call when the imbalance in my body returned. I was moving from one process to another to another. I had gone from bobbing on the surface to deep-sea diving into all kinds of emotions. Yes, I was clearing as I let the energies be in motion, but it was all too much at once. System overload!! Alarm bells ringing!!

My judgements sometimes became clouded and I was preaching and teaching technique after technique after technique. From the weird and wonderful to the wacky, a part of me was desperate to clear myself and help others to do the same. It harked back to my childhood when I used to spend hours knocking on doors trying to 'save' people and 'help' them to live better lives. I see now that was totally the wrong way to go about it. It's similar in business with sales and marketing: knock on the doors, make the calls, flip those burgers! I feel that the natural way is much better and again, I will share more of that later.

Once again, this was all totally meant to be and in Divine Order. Now, I know that the best way for me, with anything in life, is little by little, with lots of my own flow. Letting go of that need for something outside of us to fix us - that magic wand so to speak, whether that be religion, spirituality or personal development.

It's like the Wizard of Oz behind the emerald curtain. I'm well-travelled on the yellow brick road and The Emerald City isn't always what it first seems and neither are the Wizards! Do you catch my drift? Have you connected with any Wizards and Emerald Cities in the spiritual world? It's time to say "click, click, click, there's no place like home." And home is where the heart is. We all have within us all that we desire and require to clear our vibes and feel good now and I feel that's the truth.

Obviously, support and guidance is great too, but ultimately we are the only ones who fully know ourselves and what feels right, hence why I knew I had to start this book with supporting you to connect with your own YOUnique Inner Truth, so that you know what is true for you. As I said, I am simply a traveller on the journey of life, sharing what is true for me and you can choose to cherry-pick any of that you like, or not. It's all good!

Take a moment now to breathe deeply and allow yourself to settle.

Breath. Relax.   Allow.

Are there any practices, processes or people that you may be caught up in? (Except me and this book, lol! Only messing about! It's all good!)

Are there any Wizards of Oz you are ready to let go of? Anyone 'out there' telling you they can offer you the keys to the world or the steps to your dream life? Another 'good' one which seems to be coming up lately is people offering vibrational upgrades. Why can't we vibrationally upgrade ourselves thank you very muchly?

I also want to be really open here, and just in case you happen across any of my old YouTube videos, I have also been caught in the trap of being or wanting to be the Wizard, as well as being influenced by these kinds of people - ironic isn't it?

I know, as I said, it's helpful to have support and guidance and people cheering us on - Spiritual Cheerleaders - and that's ok; it's just about us knowing what is healthy and what we're 'caught up' in. Only you will know and that's all good. You are right where you are meant to be. It's in Divine Order. Imagine lots of energy cords coming off you; some are loose, some are tangled, some are short and some are long. They can be any colour, shape and size you desire. What do these represent to you? What people, situations, circumstances, spiritual or religious practices or processes do these energy threads represent and which feel right to you at this time?

There's no right or wrong answer. Simply tune into what feels right to you.

Now imagine the energy cords which represent anything that is ready to let go of are detaching from your body. They are disappearing, floating off into the distance and clearing your energy field. Some may feel they want to hang around and some may feel harder to clear. Acknowledge this and let's intend that what's ready to go, goes. Intention is a very powerful energy and when we set intentions, the Universe hears us.

Let's free ourselves up to be more of who we really are - these beautiful and unique beings. Rather than being caught up in the energy of all these different threads and cords of our past teachings and experiences, it's time to let them go and be in each 'now' moment.

I feel this is also the perfect time to slip on in here about our connections online. This has arrived in the third layer of writing this, as since I returned from Spain, and once again having a full and consistent online connection, I have been getting caught up in the social communities and all of the different variety of people and messages which are available to us at the click of a button. We can start to live through the posts and updates of others, or maybe even negatively express ourselves or compare our lives to their lives and what they are doing. I know, I have been there before and sometimes still go there. Yes, it's a good way to see what's out there in the world and to have the intention to make different choices via what we see on this form of media, but it can also be a destructive energy as well, and if you know me, you know how much I love to connect online. Once again, it's about balance.

See what feels true to you and maybe the next time you reach for your iPhone and start scrolling, stop and go for a nice walk or call a friend for a lovely chat. Do something offline. Do more things offline where hugs and eye contact can be exchanged. It feels really good. We can't live our lives only knowing people's faces in little square boxes!

All of this feels fresh and expansive; new, shiny and bright, like we are shedding an old snakeskin, making way for the new. What do you feel?

If we can identify with the moments where something which once felt right now feels wrong, or the moments where we are caught up in something which is sucking the energy from us, as well as connecting with the new and different paths coming in as we let go of the old, then we are finding our organic balance and flow. Clearer signs show up to lead the way and show us the best direction, and if we go off the path, that's ok too. Maybe we were meant to see something or connect with something on the way there or the way back. Everything connects and reconnects with where we have been and where we will be in life. It's all in divine order in each and every moment, trust this process.

For me, I knew that 'The Truth' I was raised with wasn't 'my truth.' I always felt this from being small. That said, and each to their own, as I said earlier, I am very grateful to have such loving caring parents, who always do their best and who were doing their best at the time. We are all doing our best with what we know each and every day.

I know now that the things I have been

caught up in have supported my spiritual growth and views on life. Some of which I have learnt and still enjoy and find useful I share in this book. That said, for me, it just doesn't feel right when someone else is telling me what to do and what is right or wrong. Had I not experienced this, maybe I wouldn't be here writing this book at all!

The more we get really clear about the traps and cycles we get caught up in, and this goes for everything, then the clearer they become. I can now connect much more clearly with and identify the repeating patterns in my life, such as wanting to be part of communities and with like-minded people. This has happened in particular since leaving my job, as that in itself was a community of people; like birds of a feather that flock together. There are lots of other communities I had and have joined. I am part of some of those now, such as in the village where I live, our local pub, our local holistic centre, the dog walking community and many, many more and that's cool. I just feel more balanced with it, knowing that this serves me.

What serves you and how can you be more balanced with your way of connection?

It's cool! It's whatever serves our own expansion in each moment. Once again, I will say here, none of it is wrong, it's ok, it's simply about us being clear and choosing from our own truth what we want to choose to be a part of and to get clear about what it brings us and why we are doing it. It's about being more in balance with it all, and where anything doesn't allow that kind of balance or freedom of feelings, experiences and speech, then maybe that's not supposed to be part of our own true nature and ways of life. I will let you decide for yourself.

One of the great teachers I would love to finish this chapter off with is Pacha Mama ~ Mother Earth. She has been one consistent truth and support in my life. I love her community of plants, animals and all things natural in nature. It's time to tune in to this wonderful energy.

Chapter 4

Nature-Nurture ~ URPICHAY Pacha Mama! ❤

I was taught the word URPICHAY in Peru; it means "I am doing my best so that you may receive it and share with others." It can also mean "Thank you from my heart." ❤ It's a wonderful word that always gives me the goosies when I say it.

Urpichay Pacha Mama is one of my daily prayers that I say out in nature. I say it to thank Mother Earth for all she does, her consistency in her giving and how we can all share in this each day.

I believe if we can tune into the energy of Pacha Mama each and every day, life gets more and more magical. There's a lot more on magic to follow in the chapters to come. That said, I feel that everything I have been sharing here so far feels pretty magical, as does life.

I hope you are feeling that too.

Everything about nature to me feels very connected and plugged in. Living in England, I love to experience the different seasons and changes of temperature. The lush green of Spring springing after the cold and sometimes bleak winters. The summer flowers in bloom leading to the beautiful warming autumnal colours as the leaves start to fall.

As I type this here today, I have to add to the words that I wrote in the warmth of the sun last week over in Spain. I have a raging fire going at the moment in my old 1920s range. It's reaching late September here in Yorkshire and we have just passed the Autumn Equinox; it's harvest time, it's also the time the temperatures start to drop. The warmth of a real fire after a morning of walking out in nature with my furry friends is really lovely and sometimes blissful, depending on how the mood takes me. For today, it simply feels good, the warmth on my skin and the glow of the flames giving me hope. These last few days since returning home have brought up a lot of contrast. I'm finding it hard to feel the light and a lot is coming up to clear. Lots of walking and 'nature-nurture' is helping clear the way.

Nature-nurture. There is so much of it here for us to enjoy and it's constant, always there, giving and sharing with us in so many different forms. Just like the air we breathe and the water we drink, it's naturally abundant. In case you don't already spend daily time in nature, I would highly recommend it. For me, it's been a big part of my healing journey, supporting the balance to come back in.

Even if you don't live in the countryside like me, I am sure there's a park or somewhere with a little greenery you can visit each day, even if it's simply your garden. In case you aren't able to go out of the house that much, be sure to open your windows and breathe in the fresh air. Be at one with nature as much as possible and breathe it all in. Open up to this nature nurture and it matters not what the weather is doing - it's not the weather that's the problem, it's choosing the wrong clothes! I know this well, living here in the north of England; rain isn't a bad thing (unless we believe it is). Rain is the clearing waters washing away what's ready to go, feeding and rehydrating the plants. Maybe tears from Pacha Mama? Maybe mirroring some tears which we are ready to release? See what you feel.

I believe the weather can reflect our moods and emotions and that we can tune into what's happening around us and allow it to help us to clear. The wild winds blowing away the cobwebs of contrast; the rains washing and clearing; the rainbows bringing in the colour, light and wonderment amidst clouds and rains and the warmth of the sunshine brightly lighting the way. The same can be said for the light of the moon by night. Everything in nature holds meaning.

The sun is shining brightly on the beach as I write here today in Spain, twinkling and sparkling like a million diamonds on the sea - beautiful! That reminds me of my last walk before jetting off on holiday here. It was very grey, misty, wet and chilly at home, as I looked over the valley where all the spiders' webs were glistening with the moisture they had collected. They looked like diamond necklaces and diamond hammocks in the bilberry bushes, totally incredible. All of these different wonders of the world right here at our fingertips, on our doorsteps, ready to be discovered and enjoyed. Totally magical!

Wherever you are right now, look out of a window, or if it's possible and better still, go outside, take a really good look around and breathe it all in. Put your hands towards the ground and say "URPICHAY Pacha Mama, thank you, thank you, thank you, I LOVE You!" See how that feels to you.

Magic!

I am sure you will have heard the saying about the sun rising every morning and the fact that we don't have to do anything to make this happen. It just happens naturally and it shines so brightly for us, even behind the clouds on a dull day.

Just the same as when the sun sets and the moon rises it also shines for us, out into the darkness, unless it's a dark moon, but at least the stars will still shine for us during those times! The natural lights always there guiding us. This always happens each and every day, without us having any involvement. How fabulous is that?!

There is so much beauty all around us, that we are able to see which happens above the surface of the earth, as well as what goes on beneath the surface; the depth of the oceans; underground and right to the core – the centre of this magnificent planet. As well as the infinity of the skies and the whole Universe around us, it's massive, HUGE and truly miraculous. So much more than we could ever imagine it to be! Can you feel the truth of that?

I could go on and on about the infinity and magicalness of this world and Universe around us (is magicalness a word?!? it sounds right to me, lol!) Magicalness of the life! Total Magicalness! Everyday Magicalness! FAB!

Yes, as I was saying, I could go on and on and on about how infinite this all is. Have I mentioned that I'm an Aquarian aka an Alien? It's easy for us to get carried away with the energetic expansion and travel off to other planets on a cloud of magicalness!

On the subject of the moon rising and lighting the darkness, I wanted to slip a little bit in here about the moon cycles. I have been tuning into and following the moon cycles for the past few years, and it's no coincidence that around the same time I started to follow the moon cycles, my chap was gifted an Omega moon watch for his birthday so it's now even easier to keep track.

Just as the moon affects the waters of the oceans and the rising of the tides, they, in turn, affect us and our energy. Our bodies are made up of a huge percentage of water, so to me this makes sense. The full moon or Lunatic ~ Luna = moon. I will talk about this more in the next chapter as there's lots to say.

Back to the earth, the ground. I wanted to share more about what goes on underneath the earth and talk about Shit and Diamonds if that's ok with you. I understand that this sounds like a strange mix – shit and diamonds, but all will become clear.

We can allow Pacha Mama to help us clear all of our vibrational shit and connect us with the diamonds in the darkness.

Throughout the different seasons and leading up to harvest time, the tractors go up and down the country lane I live on with enormous tractors full of manure, aka shit!

They cover the fields with it to help support crops to grow. We also have a livery yard at the bottom of the lane, so it's like the M1 for horses (The M1 is a motorway I used to live near, so I much prefer the horse traffic passing by my cottage now rather than all the cars and lorries). The horses tripping up and down the lane often leave a nice big pile of steaming shit and one of my neighbours pops out to collect it as manure for her roses.

Pacha Mama takes this gift and along with the help of the soil creatures, mulches and mixes it around to support regrowth.

I love to look at our vibrational shit like this too. The shadow stuff. The darkness with us. The bad vibes. The heavy stuff. Whatever we label it or call it matters not. We can set the intention to release it to the earth, to breathe in goodness and release that which is ready to go. It's a good thing and Pacha Mama will thank us. I do this when I am out walking each day. Would you like to join me? Let's go out in nature and purge to Pacha Mama! See how much lighter and brighter you feel when you return home.

Now for the diamond bit. They are created from deep within the earth as particular rocks, I think its coal, rub together (excuse my childlike explanation, as I really don't know what I am talking about here but love this analogy nonetheless lol), the rubbing and friction creates the diamond from deep, deep under the earth's crust. Within all of that darkness, a brilliant rainbow light catcher is created, ready to surface and shine.

I see our inner-diamonds in the same way. All of the friction that we go through in life, all of the hard stuff rubbing up against us, creating the most beautiful diamonds within us, and I guess sometimes, well, most of the time, this is the stuff that feels hard to go through. These are our life diamonds and they are invaluable to us. I feel that I am having one of those 'life diamond' weeks since returning home. As I mentioned before - lots coming up and lots to clear. Some about this book which I am sharing, how the book will be received, along with what's going to happen in our life since my chap's recent redundancy. More about that later on though.

For now, let me say this. We are completely supported each and every step of the way. The ground is holding us and Mother Earth is giving us lovely big hugs, wrapping her arms around us all. Can you feel that?

As I touched upon before, the symbology of nature reflecting back at us and our lives is also wonderfully synchronistic. Clouds and rain on a grey day supporting us to clear our emotions.

Thunder storms, as the lightening cracks and thunder rumbles, like the frustration and anger we may be feeling or may have been holding in. Sun on a beautiful, bright day, beaming that delicious warmth on our bodies, or maybe sun on a rainy day, giving us the most gorgeous colourful rainbows to enjoy.

How do you believe Pacha Mama, Mother Earth, supports your healing and clarity?

What's ready to let go of?

What's around you now to enjoy out in nature?

How is nature reflecting you?

It's all right here, right now. Can you feel the truth in that?

As I sit here on the beach, I am laughing to myself, as I have stuff coming up about writing this book. "Am I doing it right? Is it good enough? Am I rambling a load of old bollocks! Arrrgggghhhh!" type thoughts. As I feel this way, the wind is whipping up more and more and blowing everything around me, including the pages of this book which I am writing, blowing off any vibrational cobwebs of self-doubt and allowing the sparkly diamond ones to stay. Blowing open the pages as if to say, "NO, this book will not close!"

Funny how on another life-layer at home, with the fire on, typing this up, it's really windy again today, and I had forgotten that I had mentioned these self-doubts when I was writing, then just a little while ago, I'm sure I typed something similar! Oh! It's all beautifully connected on this web of consciousness. Me and Magical Milo also saw a beautiful rainbow on this morning's walk and it felt like it was put there just for us, to give us hope for the day ahead; at least that's what I believed!

Lots of webs in this chapter! It's all good.

Have you got any old cobwebs of self-doubt to be blown away? And for those ones that remain, take a moment to imagine the moisture settling on them to create beautiful diamond necklaces and hammocks to hold us in.

I also wanted to add a wonderful, and what my friend and I felt was a very symbolic nature example when we commented on one of my neighbours sweeping up his leaves into piles on a very wild, windy day. We were on our way back from a walk and nearly got blown to Oz a few times on this particular day! We questioned why he would bother sweeping the leaves into piles on such a windy day. He smiled and said "keep an eye on these leaves over the coming days, they will stay in their piles." So I did just that and the leaves stayed exactly as he had put them, until he cleared them all away tidying up the pavement.

We felt that this represented what we had been chatting about, connected with clearing our vibes, much like the leaves being gathered together and rather than blowing all over the place, they stayed together ready to clear away. If we bring together the things in our lives that are ready to clear, sweeping them neatly into one place, which could be done by writing things out, talking to a friend, having a coaching session or suchlike, then some of the leaves in our lives we would like to clear may remain for a little while, until we are ready to completely let them go and clear them out.

This is ok, as even in the windiest, stormiest times of our lives, hopefully they will remain neatly together, rather than blowing all over the place. In relation to our emotions and feelings, I felt that this was a fabulous indicator from Mother Nature, as rather than them all spilling out, we are keeping them together, when the intentions there that is!

There is one last thing that I would like to mention on a practical nature-nurture level. Do you remember Huckleberry Finn, with his red and white checked cloth backpack? Well, it was more of a cloth pack held by a stick which he carried his lunch in, but I think this gives a great visual for something we can imagine taking out on a walk. A vibrational, imaginary one filled with all the things we are ready to let go of in our lives. The stuff that's ready to recycle. The bag can be as big or as small as you like - imagine it as you please, but be sure to set the intention to empty it as you walk along; or if you are like me, I like to reach a certain point on my walk, give out a big "URPICHAY PACHA MAMA" and let go... Ahhhhhhh, yes that feels good!

I feel I also want to do a little backtracking to the shit stuff I spoke about earlier, but this time referring to our literal shit. Yes, I mean the stuff we poop out of our bodies! Did I mention that my other job is a shitologist?? Once I get going on this subject, there's no stopping me. You can't beat a bit of toilet humour either, can you? The magic of poop! When we poop out the shit, we can set the intention to poop out with it any stuff that's no longer serving us. To clear ourselves both of actual waste as well as vibrational waste. Our bodies will also be reflecting how we are holding onto or letting go of the crap too. I am always a very regular person (I know -

too much information!), but since returning from Spain, I've been feeling a little bunged up, in more ways than one. I am setting the intention, this all frees up and clears. We can all do this too - intend it, clear it, connect with the magic in it, and yes, that even includes poo! I like to call this "Spiritual Shitology."

Rather than finish this chapter talking about poo, I just can't help myself but share a little more magic on rainbows. Without the rain and the sun existing together, the beauty of a rainbow would never be seen and how rubbish would that be!!! Come on, admit it... Everyone loves a rainbow and the odd unicorn or two, even if they are rainbow shitting unicorns! Lol! Right enough swearing, over and out for this chapter!

Chapter 5

Connecting with the Magic ♥

I feel somewhat pulled, at this point, to share more about connecting with the magic of life and that very much excites me. There's so much to share on this topic that this chapter, I feel, will simply be a starter leading onto other chapters packed with magical ways of being and living. If I am totally honest, I had to get the truth stuff out of the way first, as I wanted you to be able to make up your own mind and heart about what feels right to you. As I mentioned before, what I share here is simply my experience, to support and guide you along your life journey.

I'm just like you, and we are all beautifully imperfect in our humanness. Talking about imperfections, here's a magical new way to look at this.

Imperfection = I'm~Perfection
Imperfect = I'm~Perfect

We are what we are and it is what it is. ♥

Once we learn to connect with the releasing

of resistance, to ourselves; who we are; what we are and what life is; we can then start to live more magically, releasing that resistance to life as it is. Everyday life and everyday magic.

When we release the resistance, this feels a lot like the expansion I spoke about during the 'connect with your truth' chapter. It feels light and bright, as long as it's the truth to you. I couldn't understand why anyone wouldn't find truth and expansion in releasing all that yucky, tense resistance though, could you?

Are there any areas of your life where you may be holding onto resistance? Any areas which feel heavy, tight, dense and tense?

Can you let go?
If not why not?

What does this mean to you? Maybe backtrack a little here to the nature-nurture that we talked about in the last chapter and take one of those vibrational backpacks for a walk and release if you can. Let that vibrational backpack go. It could be the weight of the world you carry on your shoulders giving you that backache. Time to let go.

The dictionary meaning for the word magic is the power of influencing events by using mysterious or supernatural forces.

From this, I believe it is forces and not force which create the magic and we should be super~natural in our flow and it's not really that much of a mystery when you know how. Let's start simple and where you are right here and right now.

Connecting with the magic of life doesn't mean you have to jet off to sunnier climes and sit on a beach meditating and 'Ommm~ing' all day. Ok, ok, I know that sounds rich coming from me, as I sit here on the beach writing this book, as I've already mentioned I am living a wonderful life at home in the country; it's what I always dreamed of. I just happen to find myself here with a full weekend to myself, as my chap's gone on a stag do. I have no dogs to walk, nowhere to be and nothing to do, so it's all good and totally in Divine Order and it's right before the week I said I would have the first draft ready and with the publisher. Totally meant to be!

Anyhow, back to the magic and connecting with it. There's no place special to go to be or see the magic, the magic is all around and is us at every single moment, even when it doesn't feel that it is! More on that in a bit.

I would like to share a story with you. Before I moved to the country, I wasn't living in my ideal place, and even as I find myself now living in more of an ideal place, our cottage is small and much more like a holiday cottage than a house, but that's cool too. I am open for expansion when I align with it and would love a bigger country cottage with a space for my coaching and book writing, maybe even a yurt and definitely a bigger garden for more fur babies! Woof woof! There are always improvements to be made and that's a part of life. That said, our cottage is the perfect reflection of where I am at and how much I have cleared my vibes.

I connected with the magic of moving here by surrendering to where we were living at the time. Let me share more.

I'm a big believer in the following:

It's not about what we are experiencing in life, but how we feel about what we are experiencing.

Therefore, it matters not what is happening around us in our lives right now, but what matters is our feelings about it all and how we are vibrating. How are your vibes right now?

For example, I didn't used to live where I really wanted to live and after leaving work and going through the dis...ease I talked about earlier, things had taken a major downward spiral. I found myself at a real low point of not knowing what would happen on a practical life-level. Due to past choices and investments in things that didn't really align with my truth, we were looking at starting again from scratch. A new life was required along with the requirement for some cash to be freed up too.

As you do, we put the house up for sale and hoped for the best. I started praying!

Everything became really stuck for quite some time. That said, the thing which kept me going was sharing my journey by making videos and doing one-to-one intuitive energy coaching sessions. The more I shared, the more the magic seemed to happen, so I kept opening up and sharing, as well as supporting others to do the same along the way.

I made a decision to enjoy life, right where I was and to start to be grateful for everything that

I did have, rather than worry about what I didn't have or what might or might not happen, go wrong or fall apart. I was scared and feeling really insecure about life, but something had to give. I had to turn this downward spiral the other way up and tip the scales somehow.

Does this resonate with you in some way?

Have you had the downward spirals of life?

A part of me wanted to run away. To get on a plane and go back to Peru and live with the Shamans in the mountains or maybe my chap and me could buy a camper van and go travel the world, bumming around. Not that I'm saying that's bumming around, but those were the feelings I had at that time. I just wanted to give up and have nothing left to give up on. Life felt so hard and I felt so much sadness. At this time, I would cry rivers of tears. I was cycling a lot then and used to ride out into the country for about three hours several times a week and I would sob and cry and sometimes wail on these rides, I felt like I was grieving something. A part of me maybe...

The death-rebirth energy. New and exciting times are coming in, yet that part of us, the caterpillar part, really feeling the pains of transformation. These are magical times too; I know it doesn't always feel that way and it's at these times that we have to be as gentle as we possibly can and take it easy.

So, yes, I just wanted to give up completely and a part of me wanted to die. I thought about dying, but I knew checking out in this way wasn't an option, as I believe we should face what's coming up in this life in the now, otherwise we will still have to face it in another life or whatever other place we check out to. The same goes for running away. We create it from the inside out, so wherever we run to, WE will still be there, as will what we are running from.

I remember one day in particular, I was on my hands and knees on the rug in the lounge crying and asking "Is it really all worth it, what's the point?!" I can see now a part of me was dying away, whilst the 'human me' wondered if it would simply be easier to actually die.

This was the moment when I let go. I gave up control, or the control I thought I had or could have if I kept trying to fix things or make things magically manifest and happen. Magic doesn't like control or want to be controlled. Magic isn't something we should work at or try to make happen. I get this now. That said, I sometimes still forget! I am only human in my I'm~perfectness, lol! In letting go, I decided to be ok with where I was, to release that resistance, to be in the now and be as ok as I could be with where we were in life. I had my bike riding in the country, yoga at the local community centre, and every afternoon, my chap and me would drive up to a local country park and walk (and sometimes talk) through our feelings.

At the time, we even discovered some new and very magical walks that we hadn't previously connected with. We didn't realise, at the time, that the far reaching new views we were experiencing would be in the direction of where we have now ended up living. We used to admire the views and stand and point over the hills and valleys, wishing we lived somewhere like that. Glimpses of the future! We've done a couple of these walks since moving here and it's amazing how close we came to the walks we now do from our doorstep. Totally magical and meant to be!

We even live on the Trans Pennine Trail for

walkers and bikers, which is one thing we only used to dream of. We used to cycle the trails and wish and hope for things to be better and for things to open up and expand in our lives. During that time, I also started making gratitude bracelets and learnt new things and this helped to keep me focused as well.

Nothing was happening with the house sale and after a year or so, we decided to let go of the sale completely and enjoy the house as much as we could. We painted the lounge and freshened things up. My chap had a mountain biking trip planned, so I decided to paint whist he was gone. As I did so, I listened to the hermetic teachings and Divine Magic that I studied some years back - a great reminder of the basics of resonance and vibration as well as polarity and metaphysical shifts. As I listened and painted, I beamed love to our house and forgiveness for what we had been through on our life journey there so far. I kept sending this love and forgiveness, softening the energy and thanking the house for providing warmth and security for us. I kept letting go, then moving towards gratitude as much as I could, being grateful for what was, rather than that which was out of my control, because I had had to let go of this control! Ironic isn't it?

We could no longer continue living there on a practical financial level and at this time, lots of other things started going wrong too - cars breaking down, electrical problems, leaks and other material things failing us. It was time to clear up and let them go, both practically and vibrationally.

I certainly did have my BRA (Breath Relax Allow) on at this time and I was flowing with lots of vibe clearing processes and practices too. I kept my balance with it all as much as I could. It was hard.

The following week after painting, loving and forgiving the house, within two days we had three viewings on the house and that was without any previous interest at all. Nothing. Nada. Now we had three viewings! WOW! There's more! Out of the three viewings, two of them loved it and offered the full asking price, which was unheard of at the time here in England. We had manifested a miracle!

We accepted the easiest flow by selling to a family who weren't tied into any chains and who were ready to go as soon as things went through at our end. The one thing they asked us to agree to, was that we move out right away as soon as the paperwork had gone through, as they had moved in with family and didn't want to be caught up in a chain. This was the reason they had offered the full asking price, so we would agree to this condition. Of course, we did just that. We had no idea where we were going to go or where our next house would be, but we just knew it felt magical and right. We were trusting the process. It felt aligned and we knew in our hearts that everything would be in perfect Divine Order. I am going to keep you in suspense with what happens next, but will share in a little while.

What I want to say here today is this: to connect with the magic of life, we have to let go of the need for control or needing to know the outcomes or control the outcomes. The magical keys are: trust, faith, hope and letting go as much as we can. Letting go to the 'Universal Magic.' I know I say it a lot, definitely every day and it's one of my fave realigning sayings, similar to 'let go and let God.' I say "I am trusting the process. I know it's all in Divine Order. What will be will be."

How does that feel to you?

Are there any areas in your life where it's time to let go of the need for control?

Are there any areas in your life where it's time to trust the divine process?

To connect with the magic of life, we should also be grateful for what we have in the here and now. Appreciation is a wonderful energy flow which attracts more things to appreciate simply from being in that energy. Be grateful and accept it all. It is what it is. It is what's manifested and shown up in our lives. If we run away from it all, often times, well I'd say most times, that which we are running away from reappears wherever we go. Life lessons to learn from.

Our perceived problems are created from within, and that's where we go to clear them: within. We create our reality, alongside divine – whatever divine is for you. It's all good. We are the magical co-creators. The true magic is taking full responsibility for this. No more running, pushing away, hiding or "talk to the hand cause the ears ain't listening" kind of vibes. It would be like leaving a job because you couldn't stand your boss, or moving house because you couldn't put up with your neighbours anymore or leaving your partner because there are things you don't like about them. Said boss, neighbour, partner or anyone's traits show up in your next job, house, relationship or life. The same goes for situations or circumstances we choose to leave or maybe even run away from. I'm not saying that leaving situations is the wrong thing to do. We must follow our own truth on this. It's good to be tuned into the possibility of cycles and similar manifestations happening if we haven't cleared our vibes about what we are leaving. Also, certain situations can be too intense to be in the energy of and leaving is the only way at particular times in our lives.

When I left work, I found very similar people in the community I had been working alongside. There were lots of déjà vu's and similar cycles happening, until I realised that there was stuff to clear within me. I had also had some neighbour problems in the past too, but made peace with this and everything was fine and dandy when we were leaving and in turn, we manifested wonderful new neighbours who have become friends - more about that later.

Often times, when we clear our vibes, we may no longer want to leave, as things will change around us. It's an inside job. As we change, the world around us changes. It's annoyingly paradoxical isn't it?

Just like me with the house situation, I morphed and changed what was happening around, initially by letting go of the wanting and needing for the house to sell and fully accepting where I actually was. I made the best of where we were and changed my feelings. Then boom! It sold! Some may say luck, I say it was alignment.

Chapter 6

Aligning with the Magic in your Life ♥

Alignment, as I see it, is lining up with something, resonating and vibrating at the same frequency, like the tuning forks which ping together. I believe that until we clear out the vibrational crap, said crap keeps us aligning with that which we don't want, and we will keep lining up with it over and over. As if by magic, the world around us matches who we are, how we are feeling and our vibes! How's about that!

Whatever that is for you and whatever you are attracting in your life at the moment, here's a fabulous 'get out clause' for the not so good stuff; well, it's one I like to put some belief in, as it gives me relief during difficult times:

It may not always be something we are aware of which keeps us lining up with that which we don't want and also seems to keep us away from that which we do desire. We are complex beings pre-programmed with many forms of both subconscious programmes as well as the conscious ones we think we are clued up on.

Then there's the collective consciousness which also has a collective subconscious. Then onto heritage lines, family vibes and values passed from generation to generation, then there are past lives, future lives, parallel lives - whatever you believe in. There is all of this as well as the cultural stuff which we are influenced by. It's a big old bag of blerrrrrr!

It's all good though. We are clearing as we go along, and the more of us who are committed to this Magical Vibe-Clearing Journey, the better it will get. We are clearing as individuals and as a collective. It's time! The intention is set and set loud and clear.

A great way to look at clearing your vibes, ready to align with that which you desire, is the same as a computer whose cache and cookies are full and requires clearing so it will run smoothly and efficiently. The fuller the computer gets, the slower it goes. Our vibrational cache and cookies are ready to clear and this can be as simple as the click of a button; our inner reset button, if that's what you believe.

Or maybe, like me, you need a more holistic approach to daily cleansing naturally, rather than allowing it to build up. I'm feeling a different kind of holistic approach coming on for this evening, with a couple of grande cervezas por favor; after my day of writing on the beach. It's amazing how much can be shared and created when in flow. So for me, right now, I am aligning with the magic of the beer and beautiful view of the castle here in Almunecar. Life's good, and as I said earlier, it's good at home too. We are all right where we are supposed to be in each moment.

I have to add another layer here as I type up these words at home, drinking a nice love heart mug of heart-warming tea, listening to a lovely song called bathe in these waters, which says, as I type "you will shine in time, *bathe in these waters*' and wash it away." I haven't been feeling much flow these past few days, so I have taken some time out. We've just had a blood moon and total lunar eclipse, so the energies have been hugely intense with a lot coming up and out to clear. I decided to take part in a sweat lodge ceremony last night to ask Great Spirit to support me through this time and allow me to continue to share.

I feel really uncertain about the future and don't know what will happen. That little girl part of me is feeling insecure and scared, but in the midst of these feelings, I know I have to keep sharing here, keep going and keep typing. It feels like alignment, even during the storms of worry which are raging within me. More about that later.

For now, back to the story and how I started to align with more magic in my life. A little something here for the 'now moment' that I can put into practice too, as well as you!

A few years ago, I started affirming that everything I desire and require is right on my doorstep and guess what happened?

Things started to show up right on my doorstep (or at least nearby). It turned out that the village we moved into created more than just a life in the countryside. It created friendships, fur babies, lovely live music from local bands, the opportunity to run my own radio show and much, much more.

What if everything you desire and require is right on your door step?

What if the wonderful things you have been wishing for and dreaming of are already here right in front of your very nose?

Let me share the magic of our move and how everything magically lined up.

Remember that you can create this too. It's in all of us, not just in some of us. No magic wand or special super powers are required. This is simply who we are - magical co-creators. Just like Dorothy in the Wizard of Oz who I mentioned earlier, she had the power all along and didn't really need to go all that way to 'try' and connect with it and she didn't really need the fake Wizard. She just had some lessons to learn along the way to realise that power wasn't somewhere over the rainbow, it was actually click, click, click, at home and......... Home is where the heart is. ❤

Back to the move. There was a huge amount of synchronicity involved, which I will talk more about in the next chapter. For now, let me just say that when you connect with the 'signs' and really start to open your eyes, tune in and take note they come thick and fast. These are the indicators, the 'Universal Breadcrumbs' on the cookie trail (and sometimes trial) of life.

When we connect with these cookie crumbs, however small, getting excited about them and saying "thank you, thank you, thank you!" then more and more will come; they will show up as if by magic, lighting the way each and every day. I also feel it's worth adding here that they can show up in any form, including that which we may label good or bad, negative or positive, heavy or light. Synchronicity is matching up with us. When we lighten up about the not so good manifestations, it can actually become quite entertaining to see what shows up. Tune in!

Synchronicity is alignment with all that is! It was such synchro's that led me to living here, for which I'm super grateful. So, the house sold and we didn't know where we were going to go, let alone where we would live. We had to take some deep breaths and powerfully trust the process. I say powerfully, as I really felt I was building my trust and faith muscles at the time. I had to let go and trust, keeping the faith that all would be well, or I would have crumbled into a blubbering mess. I trusted that the house had sold so easily after my realignment because it was definitely Divine Order and the move to our future house would be divinely orchestrated too. I am definitely meant to be typing up this chapter today too. I said there would be some gems in it for me right now and it's time for me to powerfully practice what I preach! Thank you, thank you, thank you! The Universe magically manifested me, my chap and our fur family being here, so no redundancy and uncertain future are going to blow that... It's all too aligned! I am going to get back into this vibe and trust the process! Are you with me?

Anyway, back to the house move. At the time, our limited thinking had us chatting about the practicalities of where we would move to and what we would do, but a greater part of me knew that all would be well. We were so grateful the house had sold and freed things up.

The estate agents kept saying we were downsizing, I kept saying "we may be downsizing our property, but we are upsizing our life!" and so we did.

I chose a selection of houses in a village which was on a lovely walk we used to do. It was a drive away from where we used to live, with views of Emley Moor Mast, which has always been a homing beacon for me since I was a small child. The houses were small and each had something which didn't feel quite right, plus the people in them weren't able to move quickly. We were getting closer and maybe if we could have mixed this first batch of houses into one, taking bits of each and creating more of what we desired, we would have done. Good indicators, but not the right houses for us.

It was very early in the morning the following

Saturday and my chap had gone mountain biking again, the magic always seems to happen when he's biking lol! I was online looking at houses for sale, feeling the energy and flowing with it. I felt a pull to widen the search and came across two possibilities which I hadn't seen previously. Viewings booked for later that day and one the following morning, I was feeling hopeful and off we went. The one we were supposed to be viewing later that day was a non-starter, as the owner didn't even show up for the viewing. It was totally meant to be, as I knew it wasn't for us as soon as we arrived there. We didn't have to waste his time or ours and drove away. It was like the Universe knew we didn't need to go in and view it.

Only about a mile or two up the road was the house we live in now, in a sleepy little village, steeped in fabulous history, surrounded by rolling hills. We drove past and I just knew straightaway, this was the ONE!

My chap dismissed it at first due to the lack of parking, but I knew we were meant to live here. It felt like the stars had lined up for us. We went for the viewing the following morning and it was like I had been here before. I felt a very powerful connection. Have you ever felt like that before?

It was quite trippy in a surreal, knowing and connected way. I was bubbling up with excitement and the best thing was, I didn't even have to hide it, as the people who lived in the cottage had bought a new build and sold it to the builders, so it didn't matter to them how much it sold for or who bought it, which meant there was no bravado to dull down my excitement or wondering if they may want more money for it. Even better than this, the builders wanted it sold as soon as possible before their year-end and had dropped the price by more than £20,000 within the last month - hence the reason it had just shown up in my searches. Then to add to the amazing alignment and synchronicities of how this was totally meant to be, the only reason the couple were moving was that they had just had a little boy, who was born on my birthday! How cool is that! Plus, they were ready to move ASAP, as their house was nearly completed and a fast move was required. OMG it was all happening!!!

The house was perfect for what we wanted and so far removed from what the old me would have thought I wanted. It's very much like a holiday cottage we stayed in on our last holiday in the North Yorkshire countryside. At the time, we had chatted about how cool it would be to live somewhere like this with the wonderful open fire, rural location, countryside walks on the doorstep, open wooden stairs and lots of other similarities. Oh, it was perrrrrfect! To top it all off, when we went into the garden, which backs onto a field, I spotted my new furry friends. Chicken, sheep and… wait for it… ALPACAS!!

My very own piece of Peru! It was completely aligned, the Angels were singing and I started to cry happy tears at this point!

After we knew the house just had to be ours, I asked the couple who lived here to make sure that nobody else came to view it and within two days, our second offer was accepted. It was within our budget and we got the cottage for nearly £30,000 less than the original asking price. I was elated!

We still didn't know if the dates would align for the move, but we got a call the day before to say that it was all sorted. Everyone was saying we wouldn't have time to organise a van and get everything packed and loaded, but we did it! Everything clicked perfectly into place and on the day that we collected the keys, I sat in the car and waited, whilst I watched a huge net of balloons being set free right above me. Tingles letting me know all was well. It's funny that as I write these words and look up to order another beer, I see that the beach front café I am sitting in has balloons hung up everywhere, another great sign! Balloons of celebration all around me!

So much has happened since moving into Greenwood cottage. Green for me and my chap's a Mr Wood! I will share more about the magic which has happened later.

Sharing this story took me right back to the feelings I had been experiencing at the time. This was a really powerful sense of trusting the process and knowing from deep within my heart that all would be well, that the Universe has our back and everything really is in perfect Divine Order, even if it doesn't always feel that way. This is also a great reminder for me at this present time and hopefully for you as you read these words too. The present time is a present also known as a gift. The gift of life we are all living. Onwards and upwards!

In what areas of your life can you trust the process more?

Where can you trust that it truly is all in perfect (or sometimes what seems like imperfect = i'm-perfect) Divine Order?

What if you knew everything would work out ok?

Don't get me wrong, everything wasn't, hasn't been and isn't always plain sailing and as far as the move goes, we moved during a Mercury Retrograde, so this gave me some energetic worries, coupled with the fact that the house wasn't taken off the market, even after we had paid our deposit. The 'For Sale' sign stayed up, as did the adverts online and at any time, it was open to someone making a higher offer. No-one else showed any interest and even with the 'For Sale' sign remaining after we moved in, all was well. The Universe had our back, and hasn't it always?

I definitely believe we are meant to be here at this particular point in our lives and so much has unfolded since the move to show that to me in so many ways.

One last magical note before we go on to the next chapter... On the weekend that we moved in, we went for a lovely walk and followed a map that our new neighbour had given us. She was a beautiful lady who died and passed into pure positive energy the following year, bless her. She was a kindred spirit and was interested in Native American traditions. She taught me a lot. Anyway, the walk, we realised, took us past a barn conversion in the next village which we had considered buying nine years earlier. At the time, it wasn't for us and we never came to look around the conversion or the area, as it seemed too far away and now, we are living just up the road! A calling to be where we are now and completely aligned! What do you think?

What if you could love, or at least like, or maybe at least simply be ok with and appreciate where you are right now and know that this Magical Universe has your back?

On a side note and returning here to the beach writing, I've just changed seats to watch the sun setting over the Spanish mountains. As bliss tears start to fill my eyes, I feel it's time to retire from my writing for today, but I will be back in the morning. Oh, this is so much fun! I hope you are enjoying this journey too and remember that the sun will always rise again the next day without us even lifting a finger. How cool is that?! Thank you, thank you, thank you. I also have to add that a guy has just walked past me with a football shirt on with the number 11. In the world of numerology, the 1's mean we are on the right path and 11 is my magical number. Oh thank you Universe!

Chapter 7

The Magic of Synchronicity ♥

Synchronicity/sɪŋkrəˈnɪsɪti
noun
the simultaneous occurrence of events which appear significantly related but have no discernible causal connection.

Synchronicity is guiding us each and every moment. The 'signs', the serendipities, the magical indicators sent on Angels' wings.

Tune in, open up and connect powerfully.

A fresh new day, and as I said at the end of the last chapter, the sun rose this morning with no help from me, lol! I'm the first person on the beach after waking up bright and early, itching to write some more about magical synchronicities, aka synchro's. Continuing on with the 'T-Shirt theme,' a lady walked past me on the way here with the slogan 'Open Your Mind.' Fab signs don't you think! It made me want to say "open your heart too!" ♥

Signs and Synchro's can come from anywhere. It just depends where you are looking to manifest them. I used to live on a hill, which meant that I could see the motorway in the distance and often times, whilst I was coaching on the phone, I would wander over to the window and see a lorry saying 'it's all good.' I think it was an advertisement for chips, but I didn't care what it was advertising, because the lorry and van messages kept me ticking; letting me and others with whom I spoke, know we were on the right path, just like the T-Shirt signs for me at the moment. All of these different signs, in whatever way they come, flow thick and fast. Once you tune in, they just keep on coming.

Some may say these kinds of coincidences happen all the time. I believe a coincidence is an incidence that perfectly coincides. You know like when you think of someone and then you bump into them or they call you. These are synchronicities and incidences that perfectly coincide as if by magic! I also love it when you overhear a conversation and it links in with something you have been thinking about or talking about.

I believe these magical indicators let us know that we are on the right path. We are aligned and resonating with the world around us, which we are creating and co-creating in each moment. Yes, we are manifesting and creating it. When the Law of Attraction was leading my life, I would always be saying "What we think about we bring about." Whilst this may be true, I look at it differently now. It's *our* Law of Attraction and we create it from within. What we feel, what we vibrate, we create.

Do you create lots of synchro's?

Does your life feel magical?

It's a really wonderful way to be, to allow life to be really cool and connected, no matter where you are or what you are doing and experiencing. This takes us nicely back to what I was sharing earlier about not having to jet off somewhere or go to some spiritual retreat to 'make' magic happen. Although when we are in such high states of relaxation and allowing and when we get away from it all, this kind of magic can happen much more easily. That's just the nature of life, for the moment. Maybe this will change as we become more 'natural manifestors' and like nature, it happens naturally.

I believe if we can be in that kind of connected and open state more and more of the time, whilst at home, out doing the weekly shop, visiting friends or family, going for a nice walk, watching films, reading a book or even cleaning the house, then the magic flows wherever we are. If we believe we can, then we can. I am reminded of 'van signs' which sometimes now show up outside my door, such as the 'Open Reach' or energy vans, giving magical little signs right outside my window.

Synchronicity doesn't just have to be signs given to us in words or pictures. It can come in any form, including repeated number signs. Have you ever looked at a digital clock or your DVD player and it's been lined up on 11:11 or 1:11? Maybe 22:22 or 2:22. It can be any sequences of numbers and they don't have to be the same ones. The 111's and 222's have always felt special to me, so I see them lots; as do my clients and connections when I tell them about this, so you will now too!

Sequences of numbers hold fabulous meanings too and once you tune in, they will keep on coming. Some people believe they are signs from the Angels, which is a lovely way to look at it, and I sometimes dip into this myself.

Bless the Angels! ❤

    I started looking into number signs when we reached 11/11/11 and with the build up to 2012. I sensed that the number sequences I kept seeing held meaning, and they did. 111's meaning we are embarking on a new path and the 222's meaning "keep going, you are on the right path," the 3's represent Christ Consciousness and so on and so on.

    For now, back to synchro's and opening up to these fun ways to feel the 'Universal Connection,' and why wouldn't we create these fun and playful ways to feel good and these great games to play? Exactly! When we aren't feeling it, there's something coming up to clear; acknowledge that, accept that, clear it and reconnect; plug back into this magic.

    This is simply a choice of belief system, but I feel it's a good one to have. Other ways in which the magical signs flow for me are via connections with people and being in the perfect place at the perfect time; remember, this can go both ways depending on how we are resonating; i.e. the not so perfect place at the not so perfect time... eek! It's ok though, as again the not so perfect ones are opportunities to clear up our vibes and resonance.

On the magical manifesting front, these synchro's have led to many great friendships and connections in life.

I'm chuckling to myself as I sit back on my sunbed on the beach, in the exact same spot as yesterday. I am a creature of habit, although my pen's changed now, as I'm on pen number three. All this writing, it's fab! I'm laughing to myself, as this holiday came about by synchro's. We went for a nice long dog walk with one of my chap's friends, during which I mentioned that my chap was going on a stag do in southern Spain for the weekend. "Oh," he said "my mum has an apartment in southern Spain." "Oh cool!," I said, thinking, "Ooooooh yeah, I'd love to go!" He said "you are welcome to go and stay there if you like" and, of course, it was free on the right dates and only 50km along the coast from where my chap was going, so here we are. I feel I want to add at this point that maybe because I talk so much and share stuff so openly with everyone I meet, strangers as well as friends, this in turn creates much more opportunity for this kind of magic to happen. Give it a go yourself and see what unfolds in your life.

This is also a good point to say, as I touched upon earlier, that synchro's can come in all forms; both wanted and unwanted. They are always matching our energy and what we are putting 'out there.' So, for example, when we arrived in Spain, I'd been spoiling a bit of my holiday happiness with a few niggles about how easy (or how not so easy) the car rental would be, and then I had a few worries about how we would find the apartment when we were arriving past midnight in the dark to somewhere we had never visited before. I know, I don't always practice what I preach and didn't do any vibe-clearing on these feelings and therefore, the synchro's were flowing in an unwanted direction the night we arrived.

We manifested a really rude lady at the car hire place who didn't want to accept our car hire insurance documents and who gave us a dodgy car with lots of bumps and scratches, which she said was in perfect condition. Half an hour later, with photo evidence on our phones of the battered and bruised white roller-skate on wheels (aka a Kia Picanto; I know, I know, it's the thinking person's car! Another great 'sign' there and sorry if you own one!), we decided to accept the car and be ok with it, calling her 'Betty' and being grateful she got us here in one piece, in the end. I always feel it helps to name our vehicles because it gives them a personality and in turn, hopefully a good vibe. It was 2am before we located the apartment and I was releasing lots of frustration at the time and threw my dummy out of the car cot as well as shedding a few tears for good measure when we thought we were going to have to find a hotel to bed down in for the night.

In the end, I let go and asked the Angels (bless the Angels) to support us and we manifested a lovely lady on a really cool pink scooter, who knew the way there and took us to the right block (obviously not on the scooter with all of our luggage, lol!). We followed her as she pointed out where we needed to be. Bless her, an everyday Angel. We did it! Phew! Or so we thought.

We got parked up ready to have a few early -hours cheeky beers (if there were any shops open), we popped the key in the door and nada! Nothing! It didn't fit! So we tried the other keys and the other door but nothing fitted, we were locked out at half past two in the morning. Eeeeeeeeek!

To cut a long story short, it turned out that the café next door were also experiencing key problems, so they were still open during the wee hours and two lovely ladies helped us and buzzed a neighbour who was still awake. They explained our situation in their native Spanish, as we don't speak the lingo. It was about 3am when we finally got in and guess what...? The last person who had stayed there had left beers in the fridge. Granted, the fridge was switched off, so the beers were really warm, but we didn't care, we were in! All was well. Balance and harmony was restored and we felt super grateful and relieved! I bet you can guess what I was doing the next morning. You got it! Clearing my vibes and setting my intentions for what we did want to manifest for the rest of the holiday. So far it's all good and I just realised that the keys have a Saint Christopher on them; I think he's the saint of travel and at least we travelled safely. I also feel the key not fitting, as the locks had been changed, had superb symbolic meaning and we got a fresh new key the following morning. Everything holds meaning and I will talk more about that later.

This is the cool thing in life. Whatever is manifesting, good or bad, negative or positive (also keep in mind that these are simply words which we give the meaning to) is either heavy or light, dark or bright, contractive or expansive. It's all ok. As when we attract the shit synchro's, we give ourselves the opportunity to change; to refocus and realign. It comes as our inspiration to clear our vibes and allow the changes to happen ready for magical manifesting next time around rather than shit synchro's.

Chapter 8

Symbolic Signs ♥

Have you ever looked into the symbolic meanings of the things you see in everyday life?

I believe everything has a meaning, as you know from what I have already shared. Life becomes so much more magical with the intention set to see symbolic meaning in everything, if you choose to that is. Some may say that's analysing too much, or being too analytical (Anal~yzing or Anal~ytical, me? anal? As if!! lol!) and maybe it is, if done too much in the contractive direction, but done in the magical flowing way, I feel it's fab and helps to create more magic.

Symbolic meanings, as well as Divine energy connecting with us, can be found in the simplest of things sent into our experience; feathers, birds, animals, pictures. Anything and everything will hold meaning to you, as well as things such as films or TV shows. Maybe overhearing a conversation with someone nearby or seeing something you have been thinking about also ties in beautifully with the synchronicity we talked about earlier.

I think it was our Native American cousins who used a lot of symbology, in particular with animals and power animals. As I mentioned earlier, I made an amazing connection with the lady next door when we moved to our countryside cottage. She had lived there for thirty seven years, before she died, she lent me lots of books about Native Americans which she had picked up on her travels and I learnt a lot from her. Many of the people involved in this history had animal totems and guides.

At the time of writing this, I didn't actually know which my animal totems were and I had written that I was sure it would all become clearer, which it has, since I have come back home and been typing this all up things have come to light, just at the perfect time!

I spent last weekend staying in a beautiful forest called Middlewood, with no electricity, a quirky hand-made, wooden, carved study-centre, chill out rooms and a yurt. It had real fires, no electricity and a tree bog, which is something like the ones in 'I'm a celebrity get me out of here!' It's the third time I have visited this magical place, and this last weekend was Samhain for Halloween - seeing behind the thin veil. We did Shamanic journeying, spending time in nature, playing the drums, dancing, laughing and eating wholesome foods and drinking good wine during the evening.

It was an amazing retreat and a lot shifted and cleared for me. Through the tears and sadness came the love and lightness for life. On the last afternoon, I made my very own Shamanic Mask, which symbolically represents me as Shaman Liz, and yes, it's painted in rainbow colours with feathers and sparkles and I love it! Since returning, I have manifested my very own Shamanic painted drum which aligns beautifully with some of the drawings I did whilst there, having the same colours and shapes. I also connected with two new Spirit Guides and my power animals, so the clarity I asked for came flowing in. How cool is that!

Do you know what your power animal or animal totem is and what it means?

Do you know who your Divine Spiritual Guides are?

I don't think it's something someone else has to necessarily tell you or that you even need to go on some kind of spiritual or shamanic journey to connect with this energy, although it does help.

You can simply tune in to the divine and ask: "What is my power animal and what does it mean or represent?" If you already know, or once you have learned more by tuning in, you can then Google "what is the symbolic meaning of..."

Google works like the Universe. We ask the question and it answers with an abundant variety of answers. See where you are led and follow the energy.

Funnily, talking of Google reminds me of something I used to say at my Law of Attraction talks and seminars. Try to see the Universe and the Law of Attraction like Google. Ask a question and get an answer, even if you don't want what it brings you. Have a go and Google "I don't want rainbow coloured zebras" and see what that brings you. Even though you said you didn't want it, what do you think Google returns you? That's right! Rainbow coloured zebras, and lots and lots of them! Maybe they have a symbolic meaning too lol. Have a look!

It's similar to when someone tells you not to think about something, like the old "don't think about pink elephants" and yes, we all do, because it's human nature. The Universe doesn't hear the "I don't want" part and then the Universe works the same way. It's a good one to remember!

I love the internet and how connected we all are, with so much information at our fingertips. So yes, Google things, look more into symbolic meanings or, if you prefer an offline approach, you can simply tune in and ask that the answers come from within or from Spirit and Divine Energy around you.

I had a great one the other night, I was coaching a new lady over in America via skype and her P button on her computer had stopped working, so I Googled the meaning of the letter P. The answers and meanings were very synchronistic and totally aligned with what was coming up in her life.

Everything has meaning... Have a play, it's super cool!

For example, if you are feeling down and decide to go for a walk to lift your spirits and clear your vibes and you see a horse or a butterfly; a cat; dog; wasp; bee; dragonfly or whatever it is, remember what stood out to you on the walk, where your eyes were drawn and what messages the things you saw were bringing you. Look into the symbolic meanings, because it's a whole Universe of clarity and magic which brings in wonderful flow.

I love to connect with the ancient Mayan

teachings as well. Each day holds a different symbolic meaning and each and every one of us has our own birth blueprint, just like we do with our birth charts and this is something I would recommend tuning into. It's similar to the Matrix, it's coded and, yes, somewhat complex, but you can choose to dip in as deeply as you desire. The Mayan Birth Reading Universal Decoder is easy to follow, thanks once again to Google.

I'm a Blue Lunar Night. Part of my reading uses the quote "I am the stillness that is dancing and the darkness that is light." There's too much information to share here today and I feel that it should be a natural self-led journey of discovery. It's your cosmic cookie trail to follow - see where it leads you. I can promise you that the symbolism of what it all represents as well as showing us more about who we really are, plus the synchronicities are magical. It also really helps you to tune into the energy of each day and understand what's happening on what I feel is a much deeper life level.

According to my 'blueprint' on the Mayan chart, as well as my natal birth chart, I certainly am doing exactly what I should be doing by writing this book and sharing my vibes in the ways I do via blog, videos, coaching, magical meet

-ups and talks. I am here to share a new way to look at life and also how to feel about life. As I mentioned earlier, I am an Aquarian too, so a very expansive forward thinker.

Have a nosy into it. If you feel it's for you (and you are always welcome to ask me if you would like any support), I love to do readings for my one to one clients; it is great fun and a wonderful way of synchronising to Universal Energy.

Going back to 2012, some thought the world would end when the ancient Mayan Calendar ended, whereas the calendar actually ended because we had completed a 260,000 year cycle and not because the world was going to end completely. However, this signified the end of the world as we know it. We were all lining up energetically for a brand new start and a brand new flow, this is the dawning of the age of Aquarius, the age of Aquarius.... (yes, I was singing it too lol!).

What intrigued me at the time of this dawning was that all of our birthdays started to align. I shared this on my blog back in 2011. As you know, I love the 111 signs! So then, let's play the number game...

Take the last two digits of the year you were born, plus the age you became in 2011; for example, I was born in 1978 and was 33 back in 2011, so I add 78+33 which equals 111! Give it a go and see what yours adds up to. The last two digits of the year you were born plus the age you turned in 2011.

I bet you got 111, and for anyone born after the year 2000, they will get 11. As I mentioned earlier, the 1's mean that we are embarking upon a new path, as I believe we did around this time. Every year since then, we are all lining up with our numbers, so right now, it's 2016 and I turned 38 this year, so 78+38 = 116. I bet you get the same as me if you do it for the same year. 2017 will equal 117; 2018, 118 and so on and so on. Give it a go and have a play around.

To me, this just shows that we really are all one; as cheesy as it sounds, we really are! We are all embarking upon this new path together and the Universe is sending us number signs as indicators to let us know about this alignment.

How cool is that?

What's written in your stars?

This is such a magnificent time we live in.

We are at the very beginning of a whole new world, a whole new Universe and hopefully a whole new YOUniverse too!

As I mentioned in the chapter about Nature-Nurture, another fabulous energy to connect with are the magical moon cycles; these are highly symbolic too.

I'm not an expert on astrology and the moon cycle or anything else I've shared in this book for that matter lol. This is all shared from my own learnings. It's very synchronistic that an expert in the field of Astrology actually has the same full name as me, my Sunday name that is! This was a fabulous indictor when I first started connecting with these energies. Have fun with it and see where the magic leads you.

I started by learning more about the symbolic meanings of the moon and what those symbols mean. When we go through the different lunar cycles every twenty eight days, they hold meaning and energy shifts for us as well as for planet earth, as do the different seasons we go through. Everything in nature holds SO much meaning.

As with lots of the things I share in this book, I am self-taught when it comes to the moon cycles and their meanings; thanks once again

Google and all you lovely people who share your research and magic; it's much appreciated!

The waning moon is a time for letting go, surrendering and releasing that which is ready to go.

The new moon is the time for new beginnings and fresh starts. A time of rebirth.

The waxing moon is all about growth. It's the perfect time for Magical Manifesting.

The full moon gives us the peak time of clarity and is the perfect time to obtain that which we desire.

The moon cycle takes approximately 28 days. I say 'approximately,' as Google says "The moon takes 27.3 days to orbit the earth but the lunar phase cycle (from new moon to new moon) is 29.5 days." Apparently, the moon spends the extra 2.2 days catching up, because Earth travels around forty five million miles around the sun during the time the moon completes one orbit around the earth.

So, the best way to look at it: New moons are said to be the time to plant new seeds, seeds of hope, maybe to start something new. About a week after the new moon comes the first quarter moon waxing and this is the time to keep on going towards that which we wished for at new moon. Then comes the full moon another week later, two weeks after new moon, which is the dark moon and half way through the twenty eight day cycle. Full moon is a time of powerful manifestations; it's harvest time, time for things to click into place and happen. One week after this, we have the third quarter moon waning which is time to wind down, take stock and sort out what's come into our lives during the other three moon weeks.

By tuning into the moon cycles, I have found it much easier to understand when the best energetic times are to take action and which times are better to stop and rest, as well as the times to set intentions and manifest that which is required in life. I also ended up tuning my own menstrual cycles in with the moon, which was really interesting - sorry to you blokes reading this. Too much information! lol!

I love moon magic! Start to enjoy learning more by following the cycles and see if you love it too!

There are also such things as Mercury Retrograde, which can send things into a little bit of a chaotic energy and it's said this isn't the best of times to sign documents. Technology can play up at these times too. If you remember this was the time we moved to our countryside cottage and we survived it so don't let these kind of energetically uncertain times stop you in your tracks.

This is all simply a choice of belief and what we believe will manifest, but I see this as a way of connecting and co-creating with the natural flow of the Universe; we are here within it, it's all around us and there's no ignoring it.

Just like the moon affects the tides, I feel it affects us too. We are made up of a lot of the watery stuff, so it seems logical that it affects us too. Pulling our emotional tides in and out sometimes makes us act a little like a nutter or should that be Luna~tic!

I wanted to share with you more about a full moon Sweat Lodge Ceremony that I experienced, during which I spoke with Sister Moon. It was totally magical as well as being a great way to clear some of my fear and worry vibes too, keeping my inner waters healthy and happy as the not so good ones sweated out.

It was earlier this year and one of the more recent 'weird and wonderful' things I have experienced. I decided I wanted to do a Sweat Lodge and experience this Native American tradition without it having to be something I did on a trip away or that took a lot of travel and planning. I wanted it to be as simple as possible without being a big deal. So, using the flow of 'everything I desire and require is right on my doorstep,' I manifested one which was only thirty three miles away from where I live and only about ten miles up the road from where a friend lives and she wanted to come with me too. Totally aligned!

Once I had confirmed I was attending, all the worries and fears started to come up, as well as the excitement of a new experience and entering into the unknown. I believe worries and fears are the same energy as excitement and trepidation, but without the breath and expansion, so I kept breathing deeply when I thought about what I was doing and trusting the process, knowing I was meant to be there.

Having a friend come along with me eased things too - a little camaraderie.

We started off with a full induction when we arrived on the evening of the lodge, followed by a wonderful pipe smoking ceremony before we entered. The other ladies attending had built the lodge that evening and the energy felt amazing; that said, I was still feeling nervous but kept breathing deeply. I have been a few times since and helped to build the lodge, as well as to take it down, which adds to the whole experience and feels very therapeutic.

Before entering the lodge, we passed around the talking stick, sharing why we were there (the stick doesn't talk, it's not that magical, lol! - we hold the stick and talk). For me, on the first occasion, it was about clearing any of the dis...ease which remained in my body, as well as allowing myself to regain my confidence to support me in sharing my life's work, my purpose and, of course, this book!

I had set similar intentions at the last Firewalk in which I had taken part the previous year, but something still felt stuck, and for me, I believed at the time that the 'firewalking process' was much more of an external one and that the Sweat Lodge would bring a different nurturing energy from within. I love firewalking events and they are wonderful. I intend to do another one very soon, as they always give me that 'Yes, Yes, YES' energy and belief that I can do anything and that anything really IS Possible, which it is and we all can. Yes, you too!

The lodge took me into the womb and provided the warmth ready for my rebirth. This is what it symbolises. It looks like a womb too - a low level domed structure made from thin bendy wood (sorry I don't know the technical details lol!), wrapped in breathable blankets. Ours that evening had lots of beautiful embroidered pictures of animals, as well as inspiring, loving words. It was all very symbolic and carried so much meaning.

I'm not sure exactly how long we were in there for, but time seemed to stand still. I think it was about two hours and it was bloody HOT! I have never felt heat like it before and a part of me, probably my limited human self, was absolutely shitting it! We also entered the lodge completely buck-naked, which also brought up lots of feelings of insecurity and vulnerability.

I was totally stripped bare and out there!

The fire had been built earlier on and the rocks and 'rock people' as they were called, had been blessed. There were different herbs sent in with the hot rocks throughout the time in the womb-like lodge and as the sweat and tears started to pour out of me, my whole body was shaking, even though I was SO very warm, there was nothing else I could do but to let go.

So I let go. I let go to the burning, tense and fearful feelings washing over me. I let go to the part of me wanting to hold on to all this crap and the part of me wanting to shout out "stop, let me out!!" I sweated, I cried, I sobbed and breathed through it in the best way that I could.

We did four rounds, with the cloth door opening in between each one, revealing the silhouettes of the other lovely ladies sharing the space with me, all shining in the light of the full moon as I gulped the cool air into my lungs until the door closed once again. The deeper I breathed, the more I let go, the easier it became.

My friend who came with me was pregnant with her twins and about a month from them being born, so it was wonderfully symbolic that she left the lodge after the first round and sat in the middle of two huge twin trees with the full moon aligned directly in the centre point beaming down on her. Plus, I was relived she left the lodge, as it was getting hotter and hotter and I felt it may be too much for the little bubbas, although I am certain they loved their double womb for the evening.

We gave away our fears, worries, concerns and heavy energies to the Great Spirit, by stating who we are, and in the heat and darkness, speaking and sharing one by one. I said "Great Spirit, this is Liz Green, Blue Lunar Night, Urpichay Pacha Mama, support me." Then I let it all come up and out and even though I was red hot, my body tingled with goosebumps as the words flowed out and I followed the energy. There could have been a fantastic comedy moment in here somewhere, and I say this with total respect to these Magical Native American traditions, but the silly part of me wanted to make a new name up! When I spoke out, there was a funny little temptation to say (in a booming voice) "GREAT SPIRIT, this is ' Liz Lizard Flowing Waters Prancing Rainbow Shitting Unicorn Green Grass Magic Weaver'!!!"lol! Obviously I didn't, although there was a little seed of temptation there, but it was all too intense and if I am honest, I was feeling a little scared at this point. I know laughter is a coping mechanism for me, as well as the thought of a good giggle helping to release some of the fears coming up. It's all good!

What silly name would you have chosen? Or maybe you have one already... I would love to hear what it is - and I promise I won't laugh!! lol!

After the 'giveaways,' we spoke out about what we would like to manifest and bring into our lives. This felt soooooo powerful and magical and once again, the tingles and goosebumps were flowing thick and fast. We completed the Lodge with a meditation and connection to Sister Moon. By this point, after what I think was about two hours, the bliss tears were flowing thick and fast, having been able to experience all of this and having released a lot of big fears.

I could feel Sister Moon's energy and connection and my ears started to pop and crack as I could hear her soft words speaking to me, soothing me. I knew, right in the centre of my heart, that all was well and all would be well, which is what I have always believed on a deeper level, all of life's ups and downs can just get in the way of this sometimes. Everything is always in Divine Order and on this particular evening, I really felt this on a new level.

I wish the same comfort and knowing for you too and hope you can connect with this divine truth and 'Universal Knowing.' All is well and you are completely supported.

What I do know in my heart and through the many different spiritual practices I have experienced, is that we don't always have to go to extremes such as Sweat Lodges, Firewalks, Vision Quests and Arrow Breaks to clear our vibes and get these heightened blissful experiences and connections. We can simply set the intention to have this kind of connection through whatever we are choosing to do in life. That said, if you do get chance and feel the pull to do some of these kinds of things, I would definitely recommend it (if it feels right for you). At the present time, I love the Shamanic Retreats that I am taking part in. Next new experience for me will be a 'Vision Quest,' which includes fasting and being out in nature without anything other than the very basics, such as water, a sleeping bag and a journal and pen for the clarity which comes. When I think about it, I feel trepidation and uncertainty, but I also know that I am meant to be doing this process and feel the excitement of it too.

When it comes to these kind of processes, I feel I have to go and experience these unusual activities and take myself away from what is everyday life for most people, as it opens me up to new ways of being. I also feel that it connects with ancient and more natural ways of being and gives me lots of 'light bulb moments' as well as what I feel are keys to new pathways in life. Some people choose to do things like this monthly or have rituals and communities that they are a part of, supporting these kinds of ongoing processes. For me, I like to dip in and out of different practices as and when I feel the pull and that feels really free and easy.

I've been even more strongly into the moon cycles since taking part in the Full Moon Sweat Lodge Ceremony. I've been to a few more since and have been taking note of the moon cycles even more, as well as being conscious about how I align with them on a personal level, tuning into the symbolic meanings and energy shifts which happen.

Back to the lodge... As I crawled out on my hands and knees, as naked as the day I was born, I felt SO ALIVE! Super alive and needing a pee too! Too much information, lol! Although I must say I was surprised I needed to pee after all of that sweating!

I walked barefoot and naked to a spot

between some fabulous big old oak trees where Sister Moon lit the way for me as I peed and cried, letting go of what was left to go and feeling a real sense of grounded relief. I did it! I was alive! I felt good!

It certainly was moon magic with Mr Moon Face smiling down at us all, whispering spiritual guidance and support. I reckon the sun has a face too, but it's too bright to see.

One last little note about the sweat lodge experience and my guidance from Sister Moon. I was clearly told to order myself an exquisite Angel Aura wire wrapped crystal amulet pendant from a magical guy I was connected with in Arizona. I followed the guidance and ordered one that evening when I got home, even though it was well past midnight. It arrived within two weeks and it is absolutely beautiful, so much bigger than I expected, and carries beautiful healing energies. I've worn it to the last two ceremonies and popped it outside the lodge in a wicker basket to soak up the moonlight magic.

Crystals hold great symbolic meanings, and if you feel drawn to any particular ones, or already have crystals in your life, look into the meanings they hold. I haven't taken any courses or studied them in-depth myself, but I can tune into and feel their different energies. Do you feel that too?

On a side note here, as I sit on the beach, I have to share because I've got no shame and it's funny! All that talk of peeing alongside the waves crashing up and the cool sea breeze has made me need a wee; so I decided to have a natural one in the sea and just as I went into the ocean loo, I got smacked in the face by a gigantic wave! Funny!

The moon must be powerfully controlling the ocean waves today!

Swiftly moving on!

The last thing to say on symbolic meanings is about dreams. I had a rather symbolic dream myself last night, so I am meant to be sharing this here today. As I said before, everything holds meaning, if we believe this to be so. Dreams and the dreamscape is a whole other world we can choose to enter and read into. I recommend keeping a dream journal by your bed and recording what you remember each morning and then tuning into what you feel it means or the messages it holds for you.

When I take part in the Shamanic Retreats, we do a dream circle, setting the intentions to tune into what symbolic messages and meanings our dreams are bringing us. We also tune into waking dreams, which can be any experiences in life, although for me, it's usually the ones which feel quite surreal or connected to particular energies.

Have a play with it and set some intentions to tune into your dreams, both waking and sleeping and see what meanings they bring you. It's magical!

Chapter 9

Magical Manifesting & Not So Magical Manifesting
❤

All manifesting is magical, even if we may not think it at the time.

Remember, *it's not about what we are experiencing in life, it's how we feel about what we are experiencing.*

When I first learnt about the Law of Attraction, aka LOA, and was sharing the good vibes as 'Liz Green, Law of Attraction Queen,' I wanted everything to be positive, and as I shared with you earlier, I closed myself off to anything I didn't like or didn't want to experience or feel, and I was really out of balance at the time. I guess this flows both ways. Focusing too much on the stuff we don't like or don't want and blinkering ourselves from the good stuff also brings in that imbalance, which may be what I have been experiencing since returning home. 'Lightbulbs!' It's all about having a balanced approach.

As there is hot and cold, day and night, there is good and bad, negative and positive and it's all about the balance, as well as the unconditional acceptance of it all, or as unconditional as we can be in our human-ness.

Without one, there wouldn't be the other. If we hadn't ever tasted the sour, how would we know the sweet?

Whatever is manifesting in our lives right now is ok. It's time to release any resistance or need to change or control it. It is what it is. I know this is easier said than done and some of this may not sound very magical; if someone had said this to me three or four years ago, I would have run a mile. At the time, I wasn't ready to go there. Maybe you are, maybe you aren't; see what feels true to you and breathe deeply. I believe we are being called to go there and when I say 'there,' I mean the darkness, the shadows, the shadow-selves.

The self we sometimes try to hide from, the sadness we push down and the tears we haven't let flow. The guilt, the disappointment, fears, frustrations and anger. Our wounds.

The more we push the corks of negativity down the more the pressure grows, both on ourselves and the feelings we may be trying to suppress. If you imagine all of these corks we've ever pushed down being held underneath water the pressure they are building to pop back up is massive! One day without us being prepared or ready for it they will all come pop, pop, popping back up to the surface and this can be in many different forms including breakdowns, dis....ease, accidents, loss and maybe even death. Rather than pushing the corks down if we can allow them to bubble up as and when the triggers arise then we can clear as we go along, hopefully meaning we become much more balanced beings.

I know this can feel scary sometimes but for me and sharing from my own experience (as that's all I know to be true for me), when we allow ourselves to feel it, only then can we truly heal it. In the past, 'Dis...ease' forced me to go there when I was blocking it, as did getting locked out of our apartment until 3am here in Spain. The past few weeks back at home have felt this way too, feeling like a part of me was dying, along with all of the insecurities and not-knowing that I have experienced on this journey of spiritual awakening when I jumped into the unknown.

I've had feelings of despair, of being hopeless, useless and good for nothing, crying rivers of tears and suffering many heartaches along the way. I have peeled back the layers and let it all bubble to the surface. Well maybe not all of it – I know there will always be more; we are always clearing as we go along.

There will always be energetic clearing to do along the way. Things trigger us in each moment of our lives each day naturally. We can set the intention to clear as we go along. I often refer to vibe clearing like brushing your teeth; do it at least once or twice a day. Once we start to get really clear, then the 'Magical Magic Manifesting' happens naturally and I can promise you this - it's all worth it.

What if you could look at things in a new and different way? That whatever's happening in life right now is just as it's supposed to be. Challenges can become opportunities for change. Disasters can become times of great shift, if we can open up to the love that can come after things clear and settle. We can become the stillness within the storms of life, knowing that we are completely supported and all is - or will be – well, even if it may not appear so on the outside.

On a side note, this is the perfect time for me to be typing these words up back at home in the countryside and practicing what I preach after a few weeks of deep-sea diving into some really hard emotions and feelings.

I will say it again.

It's not about what we are experiencing in life. It's how we feeeeeel about what we are experiencing.

If you feel bad right now, go into that feeling. Why do you feel this way? What's coming up?

Are there any areas in your life where you are out of alignment or not following your own truths?

Can you change that?

Can you clear that?

Can you let that go?

If not, be ok with that for now. Honour how you really feel and know that the sun will rise again in your life and the rainbow will come back again - and maybe some unicorns too! lol!

So, the 'not-so-magical' manifesting can, in turn, become magical when we pop out the other side. This is when we connect with the light at the end of the sometimes very dark and long tunnels of life. Often times, the crap leads to the good stuff, just like the manure (shit) helping the plants to grow. Urpichay Pacha Mama! It's the fodder for growth in our lives.

I have to share what's just happened during my typing here at home, and am laughing whilst I do so! I just popped downstairs for a cuppa and slipped on a huge pile of cat puke (thank you Levi). It went all over my lovely pink leather slippers that I had treated myself to in Spain! Sometimes sick happens, and shit happens too... that's life! I've managed to clean the slippers up and decided to take a well-earned rest and was downstairs just at the perfect time to take a call from my mum and have a lovely uplifting chat about how much better I am feeling and that I am here typing this book up. It's all good!

You can take this example of creating the magical from the not-so-magical, as well as lots of others I share with you here and on my videos. I'm not talking about reframing here, as I feel that can often lead to be a form of stuffing things down. It's ok to reframe as a coping mechanism sometimes, as and when required, but we must be clear and honest with ourselves when reframing, so as not to ignore what's really happening.

Hummmmmm, so what did that pile of cat sick I slipped in really mean? Interesting stuff!

Going back to the story I shared earlier about our move to this house... The crappy stuff was the reason we sold up. Had this not happened, would we be living here now? I don't think so.

Everything that has happened to this point is guiding us in the right direction and everything that comes after that clicks into place, connecting us, ultimately, with our purpose.

Here's another great example. A few weeks before we moved, I had a call from a lovely lady with whom I had connected a few years earlier at one of my LOA seminars. She wanted to interview me on her radio show. Since being a kid, I've always fancied myself as a radio presenter and used to play radio shows and tape-record myself when I was really young. She wasn't aware we were moving house, so thought her show wasn't really very local to me. It turns out it is a few miles down the road from our new house and the date for the interview was the weekend after we moved in. Bingo! Totally meant to be! Absolutely magical!

Of course I said yes, and it was a wonderful experience. Whilst at the studio, I said how much fun it would be to have my own show and she told me she was leaving and that they were looking for new volunteers to be presenters.

Haha! Ok then, that would be me!

That led to doing a really fun show called 'Fab Fridays,' where I learnt to do a three hour show and run the radio station studio on my own. It was a great experience and I learnt so many new things and met lots of new and interesting people.

What if I had never been doing those LOA talks and seminars? Maybe we would never have met. What if she hadn't got back in touch with me at that particular time? Maybe it would never have happened.

Co-creating the magic together when we trust our vibes and follow our instincts allows the magic to flow.

I do believe we have destinies to meet and that certain people, situations and circumstances will come into our lives, so maybe this would have all happened anyway in a different way, but it's that 'sliding doors effect.' Right place, right time; wrong place, wrong time.

Let's intend for more of the right place, right timings, and if the 'wrong' stuff happens, then let's intend it leads to some really, really right stuff!

Too much has happened in my life to share on the magical manifesting front, but I've shared lots on videos along the way on my YouTube channel, LizGreenLive, if you want to take a nosy and see what you are led to. I know how these kinds of examples can help to build our faith and trust muscles, so I will share a few more with you here today. In particular, a few more of the cool things which have happened since we moved here.

At my chap's fortieth birthday gathering in the village pub, his best friend met a new friend I'd made in the village and they were soul mates. They got together and he has moved into the village and they are so in love and so happy. Would this have happened had we not gone through our shift and shit happening house move?

My dog, Magical Milo (Btw: dog is God spelt backwards), came about through the most amazing right place, right time circumstances and I wasn't in that particular place for the reason I thought. I had made a mission to go out and collect feathers for a talk I had been invited to do, called 'I can connect with the Universe.' I had decided to share more about the magic of feathers sent from the Angels - bless those Magical Angels. I have always believed they are wonderful signs that we are on the right path. Do you get feather signs too? I just love it when one floats down right in front of you! I have a blue glass jar I collect them in and I also wear them in my hair and have a lovely Spanish feather that I collected on the beach. This particular day, I wanted these feathers to come into my experience. Actually, if I'm honest, I had decided that I needed these feathers for my talk the following day and I was going to collect forty or so feathers to give out to people. What do you think happened?

That's right! The needing and wanting of the feathers and the trying to control finding them meant that, for what was probably the first time ever since I became a feather spotter (is there a club or group for that?!?!) guess what? - there were NO FEATHERS! I did see one, but it was all battered and looked like it had bird poop on! Totally not-so-magical manifesting, or so I thought. You see, I was out at a totally different time to normal and, unbeknownst to me, a lovely lady with, wait for it, WHITE FEATHERY hair, walked her two dogs at that time each day. (Ha ha. Two dogs just walked past me on the beach as I wrote that!) This lovely lady smiled sweetly at me and said "you should have a dog or two walking here." "I know" I said, "my chap and me have been looking to rescue one." I didn't tell the lady, but the previous weekend, we'd spent hours and travelled miles, including being stuck in lots of traffic, 'trying' to find the 'perfect dog' and they were all mismatches for us, as we had to think about integrating the dog with our two cats, Levi and Lloyd.

On a side note, my third pen just ran out, so I nipped over to the beach shop, and at that precise moment, a dog who looked really similar to Milo walked past, followed by a couple of other cute little doggies. I decided to go back up to the apartment for a quick wee (I know, too much information, sorry!), I picked up my phone to look at what time it was and it was 11:11am! Hahaa! Fab! The pen I have chosen has silver sparkles on it as well. I know, I know - it's the little things, but this just shows that when you align with Magical Manifesting, lots of little things start to happen and in the appreciation for those things, more and more magical, bigger, brighter and shinier manifestations are created.

Btw, there was some dog poop on the way there too, but I didn't step in it. Today is a good day! I have a sign at the bottom of my bed which says 'today is a good day' - a great reminder and, to add on another side note, even though I stepped in cat sick earlier today, it is still a good day! It's all about how we look at it! Sorry, lots of layers being added here... Hope you can keep up, the dog poop was in Spain, the cat sick at home... Come on keep up! lol

Back to the story... We'd been 'efforting' and trying to find our perfect dog. 'Efforting,' needing, trying, wanting and working hard doesn't usually align with the magic. In fact, it usually pushes it further away. If we are lucky enough to touch the magical moments from this kind of energy, we have to keep this kind of energy flowing, which is exhausting.

The lady with the feathery hair went on to tell me that there is a dog rescue centre two miles up the road from where we live. We had driven past it a number of times without seeing the sign, or any 'signs' for that matter. We weren't connecting with the ease of it.

"I have a feeling that your perfect dog will be there waiting for you" she said. My whole body tingled with goosebumps - aka 'Godbumps.' Then she disappeared in a puff of smoke! lol! Only kidding! btw, the tingles we get are letting us know that we are connecting with truth, the magic of life and our inner spirit saying "YES". I knew our perfect dog would be there.

We went that afternoon on our way to Tesco. At first, I thought Milo was an old shaggy dog. He had only just arrived and didn't even have a name tag. I put my hand on the cage door and he came straight over to me as I said "am I your mummy?" He licked my hand, bless his little furry face. He looked so cute and hopeful and that was that. Totally magical!

It turned out that Milo was only four months old and was born the week after we found our house. The lady who bought him had given him up for adoption as he was too much of a handful and, as she worked most of the day, he was left on his own eating shoes and handbags. I truly believe he was always meant to be ours; our bargain basement designer doggy, Magical Milo the labradoodle. We only had to pay the adoption fees.

He's a little bugger sometimes, or should

that be big bugger, he's a handful and he's an Aquarian like me, but I wouldn't change a thing. He's brought so much fun love and laughter into our lives, some big learning curves and lots of clarity too. He's the very first dog I've ever had and I love him from the very core of my heart. What a blessing! What a gift!

The catalyst of things that have manifested since having Magical Milo could be a book in itself. I'm out walking lots more, meaning I am getting fitter and healthier and meeting lots of lovely people in the local dog walking community. I am now the village dog walker, so Milo and I have lots of lovely fur friends to play with and I've made some wonderful friends and connections. I hadn't realised what a great community the dog walking one is. He also gives me the stability and responsibility of having a daily routine, which really serves my health, as does all of the fresh air.

Milo is totally magical, and even though, as I said earlier, he is a bit of a bugger, he's given us so much joy so far and there's lots more to come. As well as helping me to clear my vibes and release some of the heavier stuff when he's been naughty - and that's only naughty in human terms, when he's running off playing and meeting new dogs and other animals, he's simply being a dog and having lots and lots of fun out here in the beautiful Yorkshire countryside. Woof Woof!

Chapter 10

More of the Manifesting, Appreciating It All & Attracting Abundance ♥

I told you I love this subject, but I was starting to feel the last chapter was getting a bit long, so I decided to start another one on a slightly similar subject. Not sure if that's how it's done in the world of book writing, but we are here to create our own flow, so I'm going with 'whatever flows goes!'

What not-so-magical things in life have led you to where you are now?

What clarity and cool things have come about due to situations and circumstances some may say were bad, difficult, hard and stressful?

Can you open up to accepting it all and appreciating where it's led you in life?

Appreciation.

Appreciation/əpriːʃɪˈeɪʃ(ə)n,-sɪ-

noun

recognition and enjoyment of the good qualities of someone or something. A full understanding of a situation.

Gratitude and appreciation are such powerful and Magical Vibe-Shifters. The old saying from when we were kids to be 'grateful for what you've got' is a classic.

To be thankful for what we have. What is here in the now.

The air we breathe, the water we drink, the food we eat, our friends and family, our homes. How connected we all are, like this book you are reading and all of the other ways we connect and share such as Facebook, YouTube and all the amazing things available online. Transport and the ways and means to get around this planet so easily. Nature and all that Pacha Mama provides us.

We truly are living in an amazing world and spectacular Universe and our evolution at this time is truly magical.

It's time to be thankful for all of this. As well

as appreciating the stuff we label as 'not-so-good,' for giving us the clarity and focus which it always eventually does.

What life experiences which have changed your course of direction and life path for the better can you be thankful for?

What can you appreciate in your life right now? Start with the basics.

Let's look at a simple tea bag, and if you know me, you know how much I LOVE my tea, especially the ones with magical little messages on the tea tags. They are always so synchro!

Look at all the people and processes involved in creating the humble tea bag and a cup of tea and you can understand why it's so soothing. The tea leaves, or herbs, which are picked, dried and delivered, the manufacturing process involved in creating the finished product, the bag, the string, the tag, the paper to wrap it in and the box it goes in. All of this along with the people who are involved in this whole process, from the delivery to the shops, the transportation, the shops themselves, the people who sell it, the money to buy it and all of the different threads which go into something millions of us around the world probably drink each day. I bet you will never look at a cup of tea in the same way again!

I know a nice cup of tea, for me, is a Zen moment and if you've watched me drinking one in my videos, you will undoubtedly know this. It's a chance for relaxation and appreciation and we can do this with everything we have, use, enjoy and partake in throughout our days. All of this as well as the natural things we have all around us too. It's immense and infinite. The amount of things we can appreciate goes on forever. Then we can add to this the connections with others and the feelings these bring as well. There is sooo, so much to be thankful for.

How expansive does that feel to you?

And notice I haven't really talked that much about the big stuff or the material stuff we can sometimes think we need or crave. There was a time when many of us, myself included, learnt about the Law of Attraction and manifesting and there were all kinds of vision boards floating around with sports cars and mansions on them. For me, my truth in the here and now is much simpler. Everything was stripped back to basics. Funnily enough, not long after I started wanting more material stuff and 'efforting' to try and get it, the more I wanted and needed, the less I got and the more had to go as I shared earlier. We once had a sports car and a bigger house and it all went. I ended up sitting alone in my lounge at our old house feeling so lost and broken, scared of the future as everything was stripped back. I knew I had to start appreciating what was ok and what we did have in our lives at the time. At the time, I had a cup of tea in my hand and I was still breathing and ALIVE!

Maybe this is the perfect time for a nice cup of tea! Btw, I have boxes and boxes of my fave tea all stacked up in my kitchen. All different colours, flavours and tastes. Now that's abundance for you! On another little side note, it's so wonderful to be reminding myself of this here today as I type away here at home and consider what we do have in life. Even though the future feels really uncertain in the here and now - all is well. The fire's raging, the tea's steaming away and Milo is sat with me on the sofa, cuddled up, happy and content. Thank you, thank you, thank you.

Focusing on natural and simple abundance. Abundance is a great word isn't it!

Abundance/ə'bʌnd(ə)ns
noun
a very large quantity of something.

Often, we can focus on money and having lots of it as being abundance, but for me it took having no money at all and getting back in touch with other ways of appreciating abundance before any money started to flow. As I share this here today, my hand wants to stop writing as the subject of money comes up, and the not-so-Magical Manifesting of it is a biggie for many of us. A while ago, when I was feeling very 'lackful,' I used to get asked lots of questions about how to manifest money and I too am still clearing my vibes on that one. Maybe you feel the same?

I know a big part of me had lots of untrue beliefs ingrained into me and I know it's untrue, as it feels tight and tense when I think about it; even now. Beliefs such as 'you have to work hard for money' and that 'it doesn't come easily from doing that which you love.' I hope to change this and hope is a very good place to be. All of the contrast and contraction many of us have had and do have with money will hopefully be birthing a new and improved flow with how the money system works, or doesn't work, as the case may be. I hope this new and improved flow which is being birthed will be light and expansive for the many of us who would love to simply be doing what we love and thriving, rather than just surviving, or having to do that which we don't love so much.

I'm not sure how things will go with the money system as it is, but what feels like truth to me in this 'now' moment is that there is a lot of conscious and subconscious vibe-clearing to be done on this subject, my own, your own and all of our feelings as a collective.

For now, I am going to remain hopeful that all will be well and that we will be provided for as required, to enable us all to follow our true heart paths in the most comfortable, secure and supportive way possible. In the meantime, I will continue to appreciate life as it is and all of the abundance around us in so many other ways and everything else that follows is a bonus.

It's ironic that I share this now too, because my chap took redundancy and our future is really uncertain in many practical ways, yet in a vibrational way, I am trusting the process and allowing everything to be in Divine Order. I hope, and I am open to this.

Are you?

It feels like the perfect time to share how this book came about and the funding which is being raised to be able to have it published. It was definitely magical manifesting!

I knew about an online site to raise funds for charities, as well as individual funds for things such as medical bills. At the time, I'd been told about an amazing treatment for the Meniere's Dis...ease (notice how I say 'the' and not 'my;' the dis....ease is only temporary, rather than being owned by us). I raised the money I required for the treatment via this site from all of the lovely people who followed my blogs and videos donating to the cause. It was magical how easily it unfolded and thank you to all who supported me at that time.

This ties in with this book being published, as I happened to park outside our local bookshop. It was an impromptu visit into the local town which was divinely aligned, as I wouldn't normally have even parked where I did on this particular day. There was a sign in the bookshop window which said "Aspiring authors - looking for a publisher?"

Tingles!

G o o s e b u m p s!
Yes Yes YES ME!

I went straight in, giddy with excitement and forgetting why I had even gone into town, as this now became my reason. As I shared more about this book, it turned out that the publisher and I had mutual connections and lots of signs and synchro's happening. He even shared with me an example of a book which he had published, entitled something like "I escaped the rat race" and that's exactly what I used to say six years previously when I left corporate. I must add that back then, I was coming from a very different place and still focusing on the escaping part but, that said, I knew it was totally meant to be!

Obviously, there were costs involved for proof reading, typesetting and publishing as well as printing costs, so I said "well if it's meant to be the Universe will provide;" as he chuckled and said "is that the kind of magic your book's about then?" and I said "yes, it sure is" whilst skipping my way out of the shop. That afternoon, Milo and I went for a lovely long walk. Often times, when in a state of non-resistance and relaxing in nature on a walk, inspired ideas flow in. That's when it came to me to use the same online site to fund the book.

I made a video sharing what I was going to do there and then on the walk with my windswept walking hair. Just as I finished and looked over to a boat that I pass on my walk every day, I noticed that it was called Mystical Sign! Ha haa! I'd never noticed that before, as I was always looking further ahead towards the magnificent pirate ship which the same guy has built on his land. Yes really! A full sized pirate ship and we don't live anywhere near water either! I told you it's really magical where I live, like a parallel Universe in 'Liz~Land.'

I created the campaign that afternoon and had over £200 in less than forty eight hours. I popped back into the bookshop the following week to share my excitement and it's been growing ever since.

On a side note, a lovely young Spanish boy has just walked past me on the beach and his T-Shirt has the word 'paradise' on it, which I feel is reminding me to share more about paradise or hell on earth; it will be a short and sweet, but very valuable chapter coming up next.

Firstly, let me say, before this one concludes, the date's set for the first draft of this book and the words are literally pouring out of me. My fingers ache in a good way and I've worn out three pens - it's all happening. It's a shame I've missed the first date we set, because it's taking me so long to process what I've written, get it typed up and I keep adding to it! It's all good! It will be when it will be!

I have just about enough funds for the first proof read and typesetting and I am trusting the process that the remainder of the funds will flow in ready to have the first batch of books printed, so I will consider it done! It must be, as you are here today reading these words in a book. How cool is that!

I have pre-seeded the magic happening and a big huge thank you, Thank You, THANK YOU for all of your magical support. We are all in this together.

Chapter 11

Paradise or Hell On Earth & The Death Experience

♥

    I'm going to make this chapter short and sweet, just like the little boy who walked past with the paradise T-Shirt on, but I know I am meant to be sharing this with you and I am trusting the sign which was given to me.

    What are you choosing; hell on earth or paradise on earth?

    I was taught as a little girl, growing up as a Jehovah's Witness, that one day we would all live on a paradise earth where everybody would get along perfectly; that we would live in complete peace and harmony, completely provided for in every way. That felt like truth to me, but what didn't feel right was that people who weren't part of the religion, or who didn't repent, wouldn't be a part of this paradise; they would be killed during the end of the world as we know it. Armageddon.

    I was very fearful of this as I was growing up, but always did my best to focus on the paradise bit. As an adult, I have cleared my vibes surrounding what this triggers in me, but that's a separate story. I know there is still a lot of clearing of vibes and clarity to come on this, as I often feel really unsafe and insecure. Let's just say that this way of looking at paradise wasn't and isn't my truth; my truth about paradise came to me a few years back.

Paradise can be in the here and now if we believe it to be so, and the form that paradise takes for each of us is up to us; as is the opposite. In talking about heaven and hell, I feel that the Bible uses lots of analogies, as many good books do; I have to say that, as I've used them too. I believe things have been taken too literally from the Bible and it's been given to us all in varying ways, depending on different belief systems. Maybe paradise versus armageddon, maybe heaven or hell and I believe we are creating it now here on earth. It's not something for which we are waiting to happen when we repent or die.

It's an inside job. We can connect with our very own piece of paradise on earth right now and enjoy a feeling of heaven on earth and the lightness that brings, or we can create our own form of hell, our own living hell via our feelings and our YOUniverse around us.

What kind of Universe and YOUniverse are you creating?

I also feel a particular image of what paradise or heaven equals has been ingrained into us all, as well as what 'the good life' should look like. I believe this can actually simply be what life is now; it's just about how we choose to see it and feel about it.

For me, the hell choices that we can choose to join in with in our society today are given to us and elaborated by the media and yes, I know, some terrible things do happen in the world and maybe even in our own lives and when I go there, I get to clear my own vibes on this, as do you. I feel if we allow ourselves to be bombarded by it all, then this world can become a very scary place to live; maybe even a living hell and for the ones who choose to focus on it and maybe even be part of it, more and more of the bad is created. When we fight against something we don't like or don't want, we are resisting and more of it comes. I feel it's time to let go as much as we can. I'm not saying ignore the 'reality' of what is happening, but rather choose to view it in a different light.

How can we help to ease the suffering in

the world? What will bring in the light and create more heaven than hell?

I choose to focus on what's right in the world and in my own world - aka 'Liz~Land' - as much as I can. As the not so good stuff naturally shows up in my experience, I clear and heal my feelings surrounding it as much as I can. A great example of this was when I started doing the local radio show. I hadn't watched the news or read newspapers for years, as I feel it influences us in a negative way and the media just love to go hunting for and share bad news. It keeps us in fear and worry - not a good place to be. When I started the radio show, part of my show was the news at the start of the hour, so it could no longer be ignored; the Universe brought it slap bang into the middle of my experience and played it three times during my show. Also, if something major was happening in the world, I couldn't ignore this. I feel it's about putting a different twist on it. Accepting what is and then finding the gifts, if any, and if there are no gifts within the situations occurring, then at least going back to basics and appreciating what we do all have in life. I choose not to go looking for it, but rather to look for the good in life and I believe that if we can all do this more and more, we may be able to tip the scales of the news in the world to be more positive, as more good starts to flow.

In my opinion, this may be able to help to transform the world. The more of us who are clearing the negative feelings coming up from the hellish creations and manifestations of some people, organisations, countries, leaders and the such like, then the more possible it may be to change the swinging pendulum.

I am open to positive change in the world, are you?

As I mentioned before, we are in a time of powerful shifts and when shift happens, shit happens too. Everything is coming up and out to clear and cleanse and we are evolving. Sometimes it can be a really bumpy ride, but I am certain that we will rise above it!

Talking about shit happening, I felt guided to revisit this chapter and come back to share some stuff which has been coming up for me over the past month or so. It's been a few months since we returned from Spain and I am trusting this book's taking me longer to complete than I thought it would, so that I can share what I have been going through. I have been led to do some delving into the death experience and allowing myself to know how I feel about this.

Prior to the holiday, I was helping my chap and his friend with one of his new ventures, which is to create beautiful memory boards for people's funerals, which include pictures from throughout their lives. These boards create a wonderful focal point for the funeral reception. They are also creating memory boards for weddings and other celebrations, bringing in the balance and the light. It was great to see one that my chap did for our friend's wedding the other weekend.

The reason I mention this is that before flying out to Spain, I had lots of meetings with local funeral homes to get their feedback and support. One of the ladies even gave me a guided tour of the home, showing me where people go to say their goodbyes to loved ones who have passed. I found it really emotional, and knowing I am also a very sensitive being, maybe took some of this energy on board as well.

Since being back, and going over these past few months, I haven't been feeling the pull to get involved with the memory boards as much - although we did manifest showing it at a funeral conference, as well as an editorial in a few magazines, which is fabulous. That said, I've been having feelings that I may have been needing my own memory board. I don't want to sound too flippant when I say this, as I know death and suicide are very deep topics. I just feel I should share more about the feelings I have been having, as well as the messages which have been coming through from Spirit and from loved ones and friends who were in my life and who have died.

I think that I touch upon this in future chapters. As I said, I am back-tracking a little here, so bear with me. Things have become really tough in our lives. What I mean, when I say tough, is that we really don't know what will happen from one week to the next. My chap's redundancy money feels a lot like the sands of time, and things we thought would click into place pretty quickly haven't, as yet. Hopefully they will, but for now, life is pretty uncertain and I am re-connecting with very deep and intense feelings of hopelessness, despair and deep insecurities about my very basic life needs being met.

You know the ones, such as having food, shelter, water, clothes and being able to pay the bills. As crap as it can be, money is what our society flows with right now, so yes we do require it to live here on earth.

So for me, living here on earth has been feeling really hard.

I have experienced suicidal thoughts earlier in my life when things have been really tough, but I have never gone there, as I am, and have always been, a big believer in sticking with what is happening in life, rather than running away or checking out. If we do that, we will manifest it elsewhere - maybe even in future lives that we end up living. Do you know what I mean?

A few weeks ago, I felt completely hopeless and couldn't stop crying. I felt like I was dying and a part of me took this literally and simply just wanted to give up completely, let go and die.

Maybe a little drama queen mixed in here, but in all honesty and acknowledgment of my feelings at the time, I was at a profound low point and was finding it really difficult to reach for anything else, let alone the magic of life!! And for a little while, even my own truth, which was clearly saying everything would and will be ok, just couldn't be heard that easily. Added to these feelings was the fact that I was in the middle of typing up this book and opening myself up made me feel really vulnerable too. I felt totally lost and very, very low.

Have you ever felt like that?

Consumed by fears? Helpless, hopeless and in despair?

I am certain we all go through times like this in life, or maybe many times over and over. I know we all have different personalities and ways of coping, as well as ways of reacting and I know I am an intense person. These feelings reflected that and were very intense.

I feel there was also an element of the energy that I was a part of, when visiting all those funeral homes, which was almost preparing me for this, as well as for future deaths of loved ones.

On a lighter note, we did meet an amazing guy at the funeral conference who produces beautiful printed coffins with any pictures on you choose. He can also add sparkly crystals to them as well! Talk about going out in style! And I digress.

So yes, I feel really vulnerable sharing this here today. As you can see I'm slipping in the lighter note and having a little joke, which is one of my coping mechanisms and not a bad one at that. That said, I knew I was meant to be sharing this as I spoke to a couple of good friends this week and shared my experience of a part of me wanting to die and got some amazing clarity.

It was actually an old part of me which wanted to die - to vibrationally die and fall away.

The echoes had been coming back in connection with my old job, when it came to supporting my chap with such things as sales and marketing (and I still hear myself thinking URGH!). They were echoes from when I was a child, worrying about money, security and life balance, with balance and security being my biggest of life lessons in this particular life journey. Echoes back to times of feeling helpless and afraid, when I didn't know about life's magic and all of this wonderful Universal and Angelic Support that we have as a constant.

It was overwhelming; so overwhelming that I decided to call a helpline and speak to someone who didn't know me. Someone who didn't know what I knew, I guess because I knew in my heart that things would be ok because there is a greater power than all of us can ever know which carries us and supports us.

But on this particular morning after a sleepless night, following a big energy clearing session that I had done with a friend the day before, I went there.

I don't think my eyes have ever been so puffy from crying and my whole face swelled up! Actually, I was just reminded of the time when I was twelve years old and swallowed a twenty pence piece which got lodged in my food pipe and I nearly choked on it - another possible death experience. I think that was the last time I cried so much and got such puffy eyes.

I am a big believer in being as authentic as possible and being 'in integrity;' in this instance, 'integrity' meaning to integrate it all. So I guess this was part of my integration to death again, but this time in a new way; having choices and support.

I share a lot online and mostly on Facebook at the moment, but in the past (and maybe again in the future) through YouTube videos. I have shared stuff about death and have also shared my own experiences about dis...ease, anxiety, panic, loss, fear, worry and all such things. I like to share from my own experiences as that's all I know to be true for me. This is the first time that I have ever shared this experience publicly, and at the time, I did say that I was going through a difficult time on Facebook, and I thank all of those of you who reached out and who have also done so in the past when I have shared the challenges (aka opportunities for growth) in my life.

So, this one was a BIG opportunity for growth. It was a couple of days before going away to a shamanic retreat, which I have mentioned elsewhere in this book. It really was the perfect timing, even though it didn't feel perfect at the time. The paradox of life!

It was coming up to Samhain, Halloween weekend, and we were also entering the dark half of the year, plus I had just found out that the week's new moon was also aligning with the energy of death. So the build-up over the weeks beforehand had all been connected with dying, death and rebirth.

The key for me was to talk things through and clear what was ready to clear, allowing me to reconnect with the truth of the matter, which was that it wasn't me as a whole who wanted to die. It was just parts of me that didn't want to resurface and be reborn. The unbalanced, worried, stressed worker bee who tries to fix everything; the corporate connector who has her tightly fitting business mask on and can make anything happen with grit and determination; the little girl lost who simply wants to be looked after so that she can stay wrapped in a warm cocoon all the time; the caretaker and supporter who does anything for everybody else and thinks of herself last, including co-dependent relationships.

I'm sure you can resonate.

Going forwards, freeing myself up as much as I can is really helping me to see more clearly. I can feel my own truths coming through again now and I feel like I am getting back to myself, connecting with my purpose, my passion and what I am here on earth to do.

Yes, this book of course!, as well as lots of other magical things. Maybe along the way, I will slip back into a little of the above 'me's' I mentioned, but I feel I can be clearer about this when I do from now on. I believe that I can look to connect with fresh new ways of doing things; ways which feel like my truth. Not the old me, who was way off on another life level. On this particular life level, I know that I am completely supported and that the magic will flow.

Ok, in all honesty, even as I type this, I am still feeling a little wobbly, but with our life situation the way it is right now, that's just human nature. Imperfect in our I'm~perfection.

Since thinking so deeply about dying, I've been receiving clear messages from Spirit and from loved ones who have died. I did a shamanic burial journey at the retreat the following weekend and we talked about death and funerals a lot, which really helped too. I also had a ridiculous synchronicity, which I think was the Universe giving me a wake-up call, where I nearly choked on a piece of chewing gum after smoking a rolly (that's a hand-rolled cigarette). I stopped smoking years ago, but have dipped in and out of this addiction during life's ups and downs, as well as drinking too much wine.

Yes I know... not very magical and not very spiritual either, some may say. However, I too, have my imperfections and like to see wine as one of my five a day when I fancy a drink (well it is made from grapes! Lol), and maybe that will change at some point too. As for the dipping back into smoking, urgh! I am open to clearing all of that... letting it go.

I have simply had to forgive myself and move along, releasing the resistance to some of the reactions I have been having and some of the actions I have been taking.

I know things like food, alcohol, smoking, drug taking and such like are avoidances and coping mechanisms and I, like many of us here on earth, am open to clearing these habits as well.

Wow! I really have got it all out on the table here, haven't I?

And do you know what... it feels good. It feels good to be open and to share and the day I called the helpline, that's what I did, and she simply listened and held space for me.

By the end of the conversation, I felt so much lighter and was going off to run myself a nice bubble bath and enjoy my favourite cup of tea. I'm not saying that I've been back to 'Liz on top of the world' every day and that I am Mrs Positive 24/7, as I don't feel that is possible in this reality and we should be true to what we are actually feeling as we move through these ever changing times.

The key for me is to feel it and heal it.

Be with it; let the emotions flow; allow it to come up and out in the most loving and safest way possible. To ask for support, to share with others, to open up to Universal Support too and most importantly to know that we are doing our best and that we WILL be OK. When difficulties happen in life, we go through a period of grieving, and grief is a very intense feeling. I first experienced this kind of helpless, hopeless grief when my best friend and soul sister was killed in a car accident during our mid-twenties. I also experienced similar feelings when I was diagnosed with Meniere's Dis...ease.

Whatever you are going through, big or small; all of our challenges and opportunities to gain clarity are different, and even though they can be extreme for some, or not so extreme for others, if we are feeling it, then it's time to honour that and reach for better feelings as much as we can.

We are completely supported in a 'Universal Net' held by the Angels, Great Spirit, God, Source Energy... whatever you believe, just know that you will be ok and you are doing the best you can.

I hope you can feel this too. Connecting and plugging back in with the love as much as possible.

Just as I thought I had finished typing up this chapter, I went downstairs to the news being on our TV; it's not often we watch the news unless something major has happened. One hundred and twenty seven people have just been shot dead in Paris, and the news channels are sharing more about what's occurred.

Many terrible things happen in the world.
Atrocities. Wars. Murders. Death.

This can't be ignored, but what we can do is allow our feelings about it to clear the best they can and then set the intention to beam love and healing to everyone involved. To hold the best possible vibration we can is, I feel, the best way that we can allow ourselves to be involved and to hopefully make a difference, however small it may be.

Hopefully, things are going to start to shift in the world. None of us can know that for sure. All I can say is that whatever happens, and whatever we all go through and experience in life, let's pull together and intend for things to improve and for the world to start to heal.

My prayers, love and healing energies go out to any of you and anyone in the world who is dealing with this kind of grief, loss and sadness. Big love and huge hugs.

I feel knowing about what happened in Paris, as well as all of the other places at the time which weren't publicised by the media, and thinking about all of the innocent people who died there and who have died in some of the awful situations which have happened in the world, both in the past and in the present, puts things into perspective for many of us. We are still here and we are alive and this life is for living. We can get through things and we can create happier, shinier and brighter lives.

I also feel I would like to finish this chapter off by quoting one of my fave singers –

Jon Bon Jovi

"It's my life and it's now or never. I ain't gonna live forever. I just wanna live while I'm alive. It's my life. My heart is like an open highway. Like Frankie said, I did it my way. I just wanna live while I'm alive, 'cause it's my life!"

Let's TRULY live whilst we're alive - and the time is NOW.

Chapter 12

The Illusion of Time Space Reality ♥

As I'm sure you can tell, talking about the deep, heavy stuff still doesn't always come easily to me, as I am sure it doesn't for many of us; and that's just natural. What I will say, and I truly believe this, is that right in the centre of my knowing, is that we are creating and co-creating the world as it is and everything in it; the good, the bad and the ugly and it's up to us to change it. I have experienced the illusion of life first hand, seen behind the thin veil from this world to others and this feels like truth to me. Does it to you?

Let me share more.

I'm not a metaphysician, but I have learnt a lot about this subject and I've bent a few spoons in my time too. That once again reminds me of a totally unbelievable experience I had bending a big, rusty old metal scaffolding bar with my throat and it melted like butter. My chap and me experienced this together when we went to Mexico Firewalking and it blew us away; that as well as walking on hot coals. Remember with the intention and the focus, anything is possible. Everything is made up of energy and when we set that intention and have the belief, magic happens and becomes reality. Things that are beyond our limited beliefs can happen if we believe they can.

This thing we call life is an illusion (or a 'perceived reality') and I know that can sound strange or awkward to our senses and what we know to be true. That said, it is possible to connect with and travel to other realms. Stick with me here, as I have experienced this in my own life and I wasn't taking drugs at the time - more about that in a little while.

Our whole world around us can be morphed and changed through the vibes we are emitting and what we are resonating with. Everything is energy and we are vibrational energy beings, made up of energy.

Einstein was a VERY clever guy!

Time is also an illusion and you can choose what kind of time you want to be on. Have you ever experienced one of those days when you have loads to do and time just seems to slip away? The faster you go, the faster the time seems to go, and in turn the faster you try to chase it, and the more you chase it, the more it seems to disappear. Tick tock, tick tock, tick tock, like the rabbit in Alice in Wonderland. "I'm going to be late. I'm going to be late!!"

The next time this happens, and play along with me here, intend that time will go S L O W.

S l o w yourself down, take a deep breath and breathe, relax, allow. Remember your BRA ~ Breathe Relax Allow.

Allow time to s l o w d o w n.

I know it may sound counter-productive. Say we need to get somewhere for a certain time and we are late; we naturally want to rush and get there as fast as possible, making up for lost time. When this happens, the time is reflecting us and our speed, the lost time we are 'trying' to make up and it therefore matches this vibe and our speed.

We are always getting a match for that which we are.

The next time that you are late, slow things right down and see what happens.

Remember the belief bit here too. What we believe will become our reality. We have to believe it for it to be true in our reality.

171

Here's another great trick to use when time's going too fast. Imagine a knob (not that sort of nob cheeky!). A DOOR KNOB. It can be any pretty or ornate pattern you choose. Now imagine turning it counterclockwise, and as you do so, intend that time will go really, r e a l l y s l o w l y and you can choose to turn this knob whenever you like. (I can hear you laughing still! DOOR KNOB! Lol)

It also works for the opposite too and you can speed time up, although I'm not sure why we would want to speed time up. If this happens for you, maybe there is something to be changed in life so you want to make the most of every moment.

Let me share my own and rather cool experience of slowing time down when we flew out to Peru.

Our flight from London to Madrid was delayed by two hours, which was the same amount of time we had for the changeover, so in 'reality' the flight we were on was going to arrive as our flight to Lima was due to depart. There wouldn't be another flight to Lima until the following day and that wasn't an option. This was the trip of a lifetime and I didn't want to miss a single minute of it!

To start with, panic set in, but then I remembered what I had learnt about the illusion of time and co-creating my own reality. My first instinct was to pray; "Universe, Angels, God Source Energy, The One, The All, please support us to catch this connecting flight. You know how important this is to me, Magical Universe! Please help support us to catch this flight!" Then I had a chat with my chap to say that the magic would happen and we would catch the Lima flight, asking him to trust the process and not to talk to me about time or any thoughts about missing the flight or it being impossible to connect with it. I got a loving eye roll, as he knows what I'm like! As I mentioned earlier I see impossible a different way, I'm~possible; with the right vibes, anything is possible.

From the moment we got on the flight leaving London, I focused solely on the next flight, imagining us stepping onto the plane. I kept turning my knob (lol) and slowing time down, whilst imagining us arriving at our final destination on time. My knob's one of those lovely old fashioned white porcelain ones with painted flowers on it and it works a treat!

I must have been digressing then, as I've just had a whack from the Universe whilst I sit here on the beach writing. It's really, really windy here in Spain and the cushion from the sunbed next to me has just blown up and smacked me across the face! lol! It's all good! It's wonderfully synchronistic for today, because as I sit typing my book in my attic room at home, it's blowing a gale here in the countryside today too. I posted on my Facebook this morning about allowing these winds to blow away anything which we no longer desire or require... Great signs! I feel that I am also being reminded that the winds were wild on the day of the flights to Peru as it started to make up time with the wind pushing it along.

Coincidences some may say, but we know what coincidences are - incidences that perfectly coincide.

Back to the story... Back on the plane to Madrid. I took inspired action and let the air stewardess know our predicament. I was feeling a little tense, but kept breathing deeply and relaxing as much as I could. I got all of our documents ready for the next flight as we neared Madrid airport and our new landing time. The pilot celebrated for having made up half an hour with the winds behind us, but a part of me knew that only thirty minutes still meant that there was a window of about fifteen minutes to get to our Lima flight. At this point, I didn't even start to think about what the logistics of it were with respect to the cases and check-ins; I just stayed focused on the outcome and I knew we WOULD get the flight and be there on time.

As soon as we landed, the air stewardess ushered us to the door before everyone else, so the inspired action of letting her know the situation worked a treat. She shook her head, saying we would miss the flight, but she didn't know what was happening in my head and my heart too.

I was praying silently, "come on Universe, work your magic. Angels be with us," as we walked out onto the concourse. An old man with a full head of white feathery hair, dressed in a blue boiler suit walked right up to me and asked if he could help. I think I must have looked quite flustered at this point and I was waving our tickets and passports in the air. He took the tickets from me and went across to a computer screen at a check-in nearby to the flight we had just landed on. As he typed in the details, he smiled and pointed directly across from where we were standing, whilst also telling the flight attendants that this was our Lima flight - another everyday Angel pointing us in the right direction.

They were just about to close the doors and get ready to taxi up the runway for take-off. We were ushered on, and told our luggage wouldn't be coming with us. I didn't care! We were on the flight and time had waited for us, or at least morphed and aligned so that we could get on the flight! WHOOHOOO! The lights were dimmed in the cabin and as soon as we were sat in our seats and buckled up, we were off!

I must admit, I was a bit gutted that we didn't have our luggage, but I also knew things would work out, because everything was clicking into place so well, even if everything didn't go exactly to plan. This is how life can be, not everything always goes to plan or is easy, but we can manifest the best possible outcomes with the right beliefs and vibes.

We were three days without luggage and everyone kept telling us we would never see it again. I knew differently, and, with a little inspired action and a bit of financial inspiration 'gifted' to the hotel reception desk clerk (our new friend); who just happened to have a friend who worked at Cusco airport, we were reunited with our bags.

A couple of other cool things happened because we didn't have our luggage. Firstly, we didn't have to wait to check in and out on our next flight to Cusco, and as we had to go and buy a few toiletries to keep us going from the local chemist, the lady who worked there commented on my skin, which was flaring up with lots of pimples and rashes at the time. Had I had my make up with me, this would have been covered up, but she prescribed me with some kind of magical cream which had cleared my skin by the next day. I also had to laugh when a Peruvian lady walked past the chemist with a spotty alpaca! No more spots for me!

Belief, faith and a sprinkle of magic and just look what happens!

Peru was amazing. A life-changing trip which remains in my heart forever. I hope to go back there one day.

The other thing I wanted to share about my experience in Peru is the illusion of a timespace reality. I promised that I would share more about travelling to other worlds. During the Breathwork and Rebirthing session in the old monastery, I found myself travelling to other lives, as well as to other worlds; past, future and parallel, where I was experiencing other existences. It felt so real! Some may say it was my imagination and maybe it was. However, I believe that these lives and other existences are true and they feel real to me.

I saw a pride and prejudice version of myself in a long crinoline dress and bonnet, playing the pianoforte and the message came through that at that particular time in my experience, I wasn't allowed to share my truths speaking out as a woman. The way I got my vibes out there was through music and the piano. Now, in this present day, I believe that my piano is the keyboard on my computer and as I sit here and type these words, it feels similar. I am sharing my music in a different way and it is no 'coincidence' that my current message on the teabag in the cup of tea that I am drinking says "sing from your heart." Fab isn't it?

I also travelled into the future, or what I perceived as this. That said, the truth feels like it's a parallel Universe. I was going up some steps onto a spacecraft; my legs, arms and body were extremely long and I walked in a stilted if other-wordly flowing way. I was part of a high commission organisation and we were holding a planetary meeting. Maybe you were there with me?

I know it all sounds totally 'out there,' but for me it feels open and expansive. I did doubt if it wasn't any more than imagination at the time, but one of my lovely new friends I met in Peru, who was laid next to me whilst we were experiencing the conscious connected breathing, shared her belief that she had travelled with me and had also had some very similar experiences.

Maybe our energies had intertwined; but however and whatever this all was, it was a super cool and very enlightening experience. To add to the magic, when we returned to the hotel where we had stayed prior to the event, I noticed there was a piano in the reception area. I hadn't seen this when we were there before. Btw, I can't play the piano, well... not currently in this life, yet I sat and was able to play the basic notes of the song I had heard during my time travels. The tune sounded like a song I knew and when I looked it up, the name of the song was 'Liz on top of the world.' And there I was, literally on top of the world in Machu Picchu. Totally magical! It still brings tears to my eyes every time I hear it.

Have you ever had the experience that you've met someone before but you're not sure where? Or maybe they've been from the other side of the world, so there was no chance of previous meetings, but you knew that you knew them? Feelings of familiarity or maybe even flashbacks (or forward) to other shared experiences? Breathe deeply, relax and allow your own truth to flow to you on this one and go with what feels like your own truth. For me, this all happened and felt very real and when I share more about it, if I can let go of the weirdness of it, then I feel light and bright and filled with infinite possibilities.

I also believe in the Akashic records, which, as I see it, are a 'Spiritual Library' and 'Vibrational Database' that we can choose to tap into at any time to gain wisdom and knowledge on anything we desire, or we can simply tune into our higher powers and channel the perfect information at the perfect time. All we have to do is set the intention, ask and believe the answers will come flowing in.

I'm laughing to myself as I say the word 'channel,' as a few friends and I have a laugh about channelling, even though I believe it and know it to be true. Granted, I can't say exactly where the information comes from, even though our limited human ways can make it seem or feel a bit odd, but some of the stuff I have downloaded and received from the ether is truly magical.

Once again it's about balance and staying grounded in this life experience we are having in the here and now. What would be the use of floating off on a cloud of pure bliss when our work is required here on the earth plane? Although the pure bliss cloud is good too, I'm surrounded by blue skies and white feather clouds as I sit here on the beach and write these words...

Ahhhhhh blissful! The sea is lapping up and spraying me with a light mist of salty water. That said, my feet are flat on the ground and I'm earthed and nice and grounded. Are you?

Just as I have done in the past, maybe you've really got into the spiritual side of things and lost touch with life around you. Balance is the key here and the thin veil remains for a reason. I feel if it were removed, at this time, things would be extremely trippy and intense. What do you feel?

Chapter 13

Laughter is the Best Medicine ♥

It felt like a natural progression to share more about the lightness and magic of laughter. Maybe you have been laughing at me and some of my 'out there' stories. It also came to me to share more on this subject when I mentioned my friends and I having a laugh about some of our spiritual 'ways.' We may be out and about sat in a café having really deep and meaningful metaphysical conversations over lunch and cups of tea, then I start to giggle as I ask "what do you feel?" I don't often say "what do you think" these days. I usually say "what do you feeeeeel?" Then we start to say (in a joking way) "oooooooh, wait, I'm getting some guidance coming through, the feeeeeelings are strong," in a mystical, deep and quiet tone... Ha ha!

I share this not to offend; I know all too well I can be a very spiritually intense person, connecting with signs, synchro's, energy and Spirit - whatever it may be. Then sometimes, when in the right mood, it's hilarious! An outsider looking in must be like... "What is she on?"

When was the last time you laughed until you cried? I mean really laughed, big belly ones!

My chap and me love to watch funny films and brought a few here with us on holiday. We watched Jim Carey in *Yes Man* last night. We've seen it a few times before, but it's still extremely funny! Very synchronistic too, especially where he's at the seminar and everyone is shouting "No Man, No Man, NO MAN" lol... Have you seen it?

It's taking the piss out of personal development and I find this kind of humour really funny. A fab little synchro to share about this too; after the last time we watched this film, my chap had won some tickets to see Noel Gallagher at a really small gig in London and the author of the book *Yes Man* was there, as he's a radio DJ. My chap told him he dated the Yes Woman (that was me). That was a while ago and now I know it's ok to say no too!

What makes you laugh?

What's your sense of humour?

Funny films? Fun with friends? Being silly?

We are allowed to be silly, even though at some point in our lives, we may have been told to grow up and stop being so silly, or maybe even told to stop having fun. I feel it's time to let that go. Have you ever tried skipping backwards without laughing? Try it. I bet you can't do it without the laughter coming.

It's time to give ourselves permission to have some fun, to laugh out loud and really truly lighten up and let go!

I love contagious laughter, or that sort of giggling which starts small, shoulders wobbling, maybe at an inappropriate time and it just keeps coming. Do you know the sort I mean? Then someone next to you starts giggling too and you daren't look at them or anyone else around you as you know you will become hysterical. Then BAM! Fits of giggles flow and doesn't it just feel so good (or maybe not if it's a highly inappropriate time, which you can always laugh about afterwards)?

There is a reason why we have the saying "laughter is the best medicine." There have been many studies into it and although I haven't studied it myself, what I do feel (there I go again with the feelings lol!), what I do feeeeel (oh no, my voice has gone all deep and mystical again, lol!) is that it loosens us up and our bodies relax. We feel happy and free flowing and when in flow, we glow!

Happy, laughing, smiling people have a certain glow about them. Do you know what I mean?

Ok, granted, they may have jaw ache too, but at least we know how to do the jaw releasing wiggle now, so it's all good! Remember what we spoke about in the earlier chapters, loosey goosey, wiggle wiggle!

How could you bring more fun, play and laughter into your life?

Kids are a fantastic example. The next time you pass a young kid or toddler on the street, pull a funny face and see how they laugh and light up; unless you've always got a funny face and are used to that anyway, lol!

I've noticed that when I wear certain clothes, jewellery or make up, it can make me feel more playful, or the opposite. I don't own much black clothing anymore. Wearing feathers in my hair and lots of sparkly jingly beads, as well as glittery eyeliner helps too. I also love crazy leggings with silly patterns on and I actually own a pair with cats all over them and some batman ones too - yes really! Dressing with more fun and sparkle gives me a lightness about life, a spring in my step and a more playful approach to life.

The more fun we are, the more fun we attract and the same goes for laughter.

Why do you think, or should I say feeeeel, that non-uniform days at school were always so much more fun, or dress down days for people at work? (I wanted to write 'poor gits' in brackets, then go nerrr nerrrr neee naaarrr narrrrrr, no work for me, but you might stop reading my book... Oops did I just write that?!?!?) I would bet you anything that dress down work days are more productive for companies, because people feel that they can let loose a bit more and be themselves. Things don't seem so serious anymore.

Who invented the suit? I wonder how many years ago it was created. I am feeling that it should have stayed in the past unless worn for fashion purposes, or weddings. I don't think people should always have to wear suits in business, urgh! I know how restrictive and conforming it makes you feel, as I used to be suited and booted in the corporate world. Never again, and that's the truth for me.

Anyhow, I digress. The point is, dress playful, smile, have more fun and embrace laughter as much as you possibly can; it's wonderful and healing. I am sure I once read a story about a man who laughed his cancer away and there's got to be a good reason why the Buddha is laughing.

In case you don't feel like laughing right now, that's ok too. Honour those feelings, intend to clear your vibes and whatever may be blocking laughter in your life and the lightness will return; the lightness and laughter at the end of the dark tunnel.

Smile and the world smiles with you!

When was the last time you gave a warm, open-hearted smile to a stranger or wished someone a lovely day?

We can't spend our whole lives laughing, but we can smile more. Something as simple as a smile can brighten up someone's day and it will certainly brighten up yours; that's for sure, and I'm not talking about the false 'masky' ones here either.

The best person you can laugh at is yourself; in particular when something embarrassing happens or something you may perceive as embarrassing. I had a great moment I mentioned earlier when the wild winds blew the sun lounge cushion into my head. At first, I felt daft because I was on my own; it didn't hurt my body but it dented my pride. Why did it have to blow up and hit me in the face, especially when I am here writing a book about the magic of life, lol! I chose to laugh out loud so that others around me did the same and laughed along with me. Like a couple of ladies who set up their beach camp a little bit too near to the sea; the wild wind waves were lapping up and of course, the inevitable happened and a big wave came crashing up and soaked them through. They could have been annoyed or embarrassed, but instead, they stood up, shook it off and laughed out loud and I laughed too.

The art of laughing within is a good one too, in case something happens to someone who isn't quite in touch with laughter being the best medicine theory.

It's another bright and sunny day here in Spain and I am up bright and early to do some backtracking about how we were led to a super fab few hours on the beach, laughing like little kids without a care in the world and I wanted to share the story of what happened with you.

It all started with stuff going 'wrong.' I question now whether it was really going wrong or whether it was actually going right; believing that everything is in Divine Order and just as it should be. We had left it nearly twenty four hours before going back to get our hire car, which my chap had parked some distance away when he returned from his stag party. Betty, as we named her (as I mentioned in a previous chapter, I believe it's always good to name cars, as they then seem to take on a magical life of their own and make sure we have safe travels), was parked, without us realising, in a 'pay to park area:' double blue lines rather than single.

Looking back, we kept getting nudges from the Universe to go back to the car sooner than we had, but we didn't tune into this. Oops! By the time we got to Betty, the thinking people's car, she had a ticket under the windscreen wiper and we were too late! The ticket was in Spanish and we'd been saying that one day we would learn the lingo, as not many people speak English here, and this was the time when we needed it most.

On a side note, back here in the blustery and cold countryside of England, I have just booked our flights to go back to the apartment next April for my chap's birthday. I manifested them super cheap and with great flight times too! We will be learning Spanish for this particular trip! Oh, our friends have already confirmed that there are lots of sets of the right keys, and of course, this time, we know how to get there. When you've done something once, it's always easier the next time.

Back to the ticket... All I could make out was a sixty euro fine! I bet you are wondering how this led us to so much laughter and all of those lovely light feelings, so let me share more.

My chap was absolutely gutted! I felt ok about the situation, as it wasn't a life or death kind of thing; it was just a little bit of a frustration and a bit disappointing that we had this challenge to overcome. A good reminder and it's a super important one to remember when connecting with life's magic that challenges are opportunities; opportunities to learn and grow and eventually glow. I feel that we, as human beings (and sometimes human doings), actually like a challenge or maybe even thrive off it! It keeps us alive and gives us a purpose in some way. See what it feels like to you in your life.

This was particularly true for me here on this chilling out, relaxing and maxing out beach break. I know I have my book here to write, but not much else to get my brain ticking over. The writing is just flowing naturally anyway, so Betty's parking ticket almost jolted me into action. That said, I wasn't really feeling inspired to start with, as we wandered the streets aimlessly looking for a police station to try (try being the operative word) to find some help.

Then we remembered that in a local shop, we had met a lovely guy who spoke great English and went to see him for another can of pop and some support. He wasn't there when we went back; but instead, there was a lovely lady whose English was ok, but not great. She seemed to be saying that if we went to the ticket machine within three days of being issued the ticket and punched in the number on the ticket, we could pay a smaller amount rather than the full fine. At that moment, a guy who spoke great English walked into the shop and as he had experienced one of the parking tickets first hand, he was able to explain in detail what we needed to do and off we went!

Unfortunately (or maybe fortunately? still not sure on this one), we had now passed the three hours (not three days) where they allow you to pay a much smaller seven euro fine. Duck it! What a shame!

I decided to let go and said it mattered not what the outcome was and as I said earlier, I was writing my chapter about laughter and would have fun regardless of this situation. It also helped me to recognise how much I had changed, as I know that the 'old me' would have been stressed out and upset and would have most likely let this incident spoil the whole day. Have you ever done that?

You see, we had booked this holiday as cheaply as possible with our given circumstances and wanted to keep it that way. Although I should mention here that it was a rear-end bump in our car at home, which paid a healthy insurance that helped to pay for this holiday and our euro's, something good always comes from something 'bad,' if we believe so.

So we decided to enjoy the walk out to possibly locate a police station in town. We felt the parking ticket office would be there (notice I said 'possibly' locate the station. We weren't desperately trying to 'find,' as in when we try to find something that remains lost or out of our reach).

There were a few signs; practical ones as in street signs; as well as some more angelic ones, as we wandered around town. There were lots of feathers on our path and lots more T-shirt signs; thank you Universe! I knew all would be well. One T-shirt said 'Chill Out' and another one 'City of Angels.'

This challenge/opportunity gave me a mission. A mission to magically manifest the best possible outcome, similar to the one we had experienced in Peru when our luggage was three days behind us; I knew the magic would happen and loved experiencing how wonderfully everything can work out.

We found it! I had to laugh as we arrived as it was closed for siesta time. At least we now knew where it was for the following day, and after all of that, we were ready for a nice cold beer. My chap's not normally too fussed about the beach, but he was well ready to kick back and relax, so with beach chairs and beers in hand, off we went. The wind had picked up again and the waves were massive. We had such a laugh 'people watching,' wondering if they would get soaked through and splashed whilst walking by.

"Wouldn't it be funny if a huge wave splashed that couple stood appreciating the view," said my chap (he's a powerful manifestor without always realising it). The wave didn't get THEM, but... we decided to stand in the sea and paddle at the water's edge, and what do you think happened? That's right! The big waves got us and we were absolutely soaked, as were all of our clothes. Uncontrollable laughter followed and because we were soaked anyway, we decided to stick around and play, laugh and have as much fun as possible!

This, in turn, led to a fantastic night and the good vibes were flowing. Before Betty got the ticket we had had different plans too. The 'going wrong' stuff created the 'going right' stuff and brought in lots of the kind of laughing that I'd been writing about earlier that day. It changed our direction.

What if this was always the case?

What this really means is that we can chill out about the crappy stuff and simply go with the flow. Coming from a more easygoing "ahhh well, a parking ticket; I'm sure it will lead to something good" kind of way or "what a shame we were rear-ended, but at least no one was seriously hurt and I'm sure it will lead to something good like a free holiday."

Not that a parking ticket is that much of a big deal to survive from, but you know what I mean, and it's a good example of how we can shift our perception.

When I used to be really ill with Meniere's dis...ease, and once I felt human again and could see properly, hear again and had stopped puking, and most importantly, had my balance back, I felt a real sense of elation.

I'm alive! I'm still here! All is well! Fun, play and lots of laughter always followed in those times of relief.

Have you ever had situations like that in your life?

I guess it's the survival instinct.

A fab film which shares this is *The Impossible* (I'm~possible) about the Tsunami in Thailand back in 2004. It has one of my fave actors, Ewan McGregor in it (ooooh, the sexy Scottish looker that he is... Ewan, if you are reading this book, I'm a huge fan of yours, lol!).

If you haven't seen it, I highly recommend that you watch it, and, if you have, maybe watch it again in a different way. It's a story of survival and hope and it will allow you to have a good old cry too, as well as eventually feeling the kind of elation the survivors of that disaster did too. I won't say anymore as I don't want to be a film spoiler.

Talking about films, this leads me perfectly into the next chapter, where I would like to share more about the movie of life that we create.

For now, it's time to get ready to go and sort out Betty's parking ticket.

Yesterday, I also said that I would like to learn Spanish, and now, I am with a little phrase book in hand and a piece of paper ready to write down what I would like to explain to the parking ticket office about our predicament to hopefully get the best possible outcome. Ideally, the seven euros payment, but if it's the full amount, then so be it. It was well worth it for the day it led onto. So, maybe the point to make on this whole subject is this...

Have all of life's ups and downs been worth it, for what they ultimately led us to in life?

I believe so and I hope it's the same for you.

Chapter 14

The Movie of Life & Playing the Game ♥

Life is like a movie and we are all the script writers, directors, players, actors and actresses, alongside Divine Order or 'not-so-divine' order, depending on what kind of movie you choose to live out.

Is your life like a box of chocolates where you never know what you're going to get next?

(Sorry, I couldn't resist a film quote!) What kind of movie are you living in? Is it maybe a rom -com; a drama; a horror; a romance; a comedy or an action film?

What kind of role are you playing?

Who else have you put in the movie of life with you? Goodies or baddies?

What kind of life movie would you like to be living in?

Remember everyone else is playing out their

own movie as well and we choose to be a part of that too - different characters popping in and out of different scenes. It doesn't just have to be films; if you prefer, you could think of it as a theatre play or a book. Any kind of script.

It's all about connecting with the energy of co- creating our own realities, co-creating with this Magical Universe. I guess that takes a little of the heat off us; maybe we are co-directors and co-script writers and then there are all the other people around us doing the same as well; although some believe we put them into our experience as well and maybe that's true.

A number of years ago, I coached a wonderful lady who wanted to meet the love of her life. After talking about her current movie of life, which certainly wasn't taken from a romance novel, I recommended that she write a script; a love story about her future experience of meeting her ideal partner. I asked her to include as many juicy details as she could muster up, with lots of feelings and emotions in there too. The most important thing was that she had fun writing it and was creative and playful about the script.

I spoke to her around six months later and she was excited to share that she'd met a wonderful chap and they were getting married. She felt the way she did in her script and they met in a very synchronistic and quite similar way to that which she had written about.

Our movie scripts can be written for any part of our lives. It can be a 'happily ever after' for anything we choose, but what I will say here is to keep it believable for yourself, but not too restrictive. Only you will know what feels right for you, so trust your vibes.

For the example I gave with the relationship script, I would start with where you are in the here and now and share how you feel about that, not having the relationship or not having X Y and Z, depending upon what you are scripting out in your life. You can even add in past examples of when you had a relationship or a similar X Y or Z experience and how it felt, sharing what's worked in the past and what felt right about it. I find it easier to write these kinds of 'Magical Manifesting Scripts' in the third person, so that you can get more creative.

For example, I would write: "Liz was feeling really 'lackful' and disappointed that she still hadn't been able to visit Hawaii and swim with the dolphins. It's something that she has wanted to do her entire life and she just didn't know how it was ever going to happen. She would daydream about being there and feel excited about the possibility of it happening. Liz had always felt like she was meant to be there, she had a calling..." (You can add as much detail and as many feelings as you like. I'm just keeping this one short and sweet by way of example). Btw, have you seen *Stranger than Fiction*? Another great film! I write my scripts like the narrator in that film - watch it if you haven't yet seen it!

"Liz always believed that one good thing would lead to another and that anything was possible if you believed. She had always loved to write and knew it was her calling to write books..." (It's also great to bring other things into the story which you would love to happen in life, allowing those things to lead onto the main magic you started with - get creative and let it flow).

"So Liz did just that. She wrote and she wrote and she wrote and she loved it! She was also grateful to be writing her book on the beach, bringing her the feelings of being closer to her trip to Hawaii, even though for the moment she was only in Spain; this mattered not, she was grateful and appreciated right where she was.

Upon completion, her book was totally magical and soon spread all over the world. The feedback she received was amazing and lives were being transformed, as people connected with the magic she shared on each page. This led to lots of new and exciting opportunities in Liz's life..." (I would add lots more details here, as well as the feelings and excitement that this all created).

"One morning, Liz received a message from a lovely person who ran retreats in Hawaii. They had read her book *"Connecting with Your Inner Truth and Everyday Magic"* and wanted to invite her to take part in one of their Hawaiian retreats to share more about the book on an 'all-expenses -paid' trip and her chap could come too!

Y   E   S   S   S   S   S   S   S!
WHOOOHOOOOO!
...and of course she said YES!

Btw, if you are a chap or chapette in Hawaii and you are reading this, I would love to come and visit and I am ready! lol

This was just a little example so you can see how it works and get the gist of what kinds of things you can pre-seed in this way.

Whilst I was writing this script, what do you think I was doing?

I was going there in my imagination. I was taken to the feeling place and I was and am getting very excited about the thought of being invited to Hawaii. In a few instances, I went general too, as I wasn't sure if it would be a man or a woman who would contact me, so I said person. You can also use more general stuff if you don't feel fully comfortable or believe what you are writing could come true. Although I will say here, remember that anything IS possible. Impossible = I'm~Possible.

Believe it. See it. And all of all of that good stuff.

You don't even have to write the scripts out, although I have found that by writing it, it seems to add a certain kind of power to what your imaginings are. You can choose others ways to pre-seed. You may prefer to paint a picture of the future you, maybe in Hawaii on the beach? You may write a poem or a song about the future you and what you are doing, how you are feeling etc.

Do whatever feels right to you.

You can also use these ways with words

when you speak with others in conversations and bring in the things that you would love to do and how you would love your life to be.

Just watch the sychros start to flow.

I've had lots of connections with Hawaii lately and when someone mentions they have been or are going there, I say "OOOOOoooh yes, I would love to visit Hawaii!" or "I love the thought of being in Hawaii!"

I've also just realised I watched a film that was set in Hawaii a few nights back too! And back home typing this up, I have also had a number of connections with Hawaii over the last few days; people posting on Facebook that they are going there and asking for interesting places to visit, as well as another connection running a retreat there right now. Rather than feeling disappointed or jealous that they are going and I'm not, I choose to feel excited by the indicators that these kinds of serendipities are giving me, letting me know that I am on the right track. Thank you, thank you, thank you!

Here's another example, so you know exactly what I mean. If it was a relationship you were in the process of manifesting, talk about your ideals and what you would love with friends and in conversations. Celebrate others who have great relationships, smile and be happy when you see people walking down the street holding hands or being happy together. Rather than feeling disappointed, be pleased with the 'Universal Breadcrumbs' leading you to your ideal relationship or the X Y Z which you desire. Whatever it is, it matters not; just start to give a different vibe about everything and watch the magic happen.

Seeing that I'm talking about writing, I feel it's the perfect opportunity to share more about one young chap who knew all about faith and hope in the magical sense. He was written into a wonderful book, and his name is Charlie; the book is *'Charlie and the Chocolate Factory;'* what an amazing script that is, as are many of the books, films and plays! I'm sure you will have read it, or had it read to you as a child, or maybe you have seen the film or the remake with Johnny Depp. If you haven't, why not? Johnny Depp and chocolate all mixed into one amazing film! Why wouldn't you watch it? lol!

It was one of my favourite childhood stories and it resonated with me so much, as I'm sure it did with many other kids and adults too.

I would like you to take a moment to remember the characters in the story and how each one represents a part of us, mirroring how we can be.

I feel most films are like this; they are also a wonderful way to connect to Universal Energy and plug into what we require at any given time.

I'm going to ask you to focus on two of the characters here today; obviously the wonderful and humble Charlie himself, bless little Charlie Bucket; and I would also like you to focus on Veruca Salt. Even her name feels like salt in some kind of wound - do you know what I mean?

Charlie is such a soft and loving boy, emitting a powerful light regardless of his dire situation; Veruca is a demanding, high-maintenance little girl who, just by even seeing her in the film, can bring tension and irritation into our bodies.

Veruca's father mollycoddles her and gives her whatever she wants or demands at whatever cost.

"DADDY I WANT A GOLDEN TICKET!!!!!" "I WANT, I WANT, I WANT!!!!"

It's ironic that, by the end of her trip to the

chocolate factory, she's deemed a bad nut by the squirrels and sent down the rubbish shoot!

Charlie, on the other hand, really, really wants a Golden Ticket, but he has no one to demand it from and I don't even think he could demand if he tried, bless him!

Grandpa Jo and family are all in bed at home eating (or should that be drinking) cabbage soup, but they are happy with their lot in life.

On the other side of the fence, Veruca (apt name don't you think?) acts like she has salt in her many wounds, although she has so much.

Charlie wishes hopes and dreams about the Golden Ticket whilst he walks past the chocolate factory each morning, smelling the warm, sweet chocolatey air and sending out his wishes. At this point, you can really connect with him, knowing that even a simple chocolate bar would be enough for his appreciation to flow abundantly. Charlie is connecting with Spirit; with his Inner Spirit and the Universal Magic all around.

Meanwhile, back at the nut shelling factory, poor old Mr. Salt or 'daddy,' has his full factory of ladies shelling thousands of chocolate bars to 'try' and find one of the elusive Golden Tickets for little madam. They work around the clock, so many hours, so much work and expense.

Back to Charlie, the sweetest of boys that he is. It's his birthday and on each birthday, he is gifted one very lonely looking chocolate bar. He knew this one was coming and it's one pressure filled Wonka bar. You can feel the tension in this bar of chocolate, there's so much riding on it and all of his grandparents and parents really, really want there to be a Golden Ticket. The pressure is on.

Sound familiar?

Have you ever tried to manifest your version of a Golden Ticket?

He's dreamed so much of opening up this Whipple Scrumptious Fudgemallow Delight to see the golden glimmer of hope shining back at him, to no avail. There is no Golden Ticket. So he does what Charlie has done so well all of his life; he covers up his disappointment, smiles, says that it's ok, at least he still has the delicious chocolate bar to enjoy and that he will. Grandpa Jo feels his pain and uses some of his savings to buy Charlie another chocolate bar with the same results. The combined desperation simply pushes it away.

You can see he still has a tiny glimmer of hope remaining, but he pushes it down, so as not to cause too much upset to himself or his family, who are all doing their best in a difficult situation. Bless him! And bless us too, as Charlie reflects that part of us, as sadly does Veruca Salt! EEEEK!

'Daddy' gets Veruca Salt the Golden Ticket eventually.

Is she grateful?

What do you think?

Does she make the most of it?

What do you feel?

As the story goes, the last ticket has been found, but unbeknown to Charlie, it was by a fraudster. As Charlie weaves his way home through the busy grey streets, with his little grey hungry body, he still looks happy with his lot in life. At this point, he looks down to see the shining glint of a silver coin in the gutter and you can feel the energy of this moment. It makes you tingle as he collects it up and skips into the nearest sweet shop, ordering the biggest bar of chocolate that he possibly can and snaffling it down at the speed of light.

As he leaves the sweet shop, a spark of inspiration gives him the urge to go back into the shop and get a bar for Grandpa Jo, who did give up his savings as a last-ditch attempt to win a Golden Ticket for Charlie. He picks a plain old regular Wonka Bar, at which point, people outside are starting to talk about the fraudster who claimed to have the final ticket.

Charlie hears them, eyes twinkling as he starts to peel back the wrapper and slowly but surely, there's a golden glimmer. There it is shining back up at him! The Golden Ticket!

WHOOHOOO! This is it!!
"I've got a Golden Ticket!!!"

The rush of excitement is magical as he trips off along the lane to share the fabulous news.

What would it take to be more Charlie? How can we embrace this magical energy?

As you already know, the end of the story doesn't work out too well for Veruca, or any of the other Golden Ticket holders and yes, Charlie has his life lessons along the way, but what an incredible journey he has!

Charlie manifested the Golden Ticket the magical way.

The magical way wasn't through wanting and demanding, working and striving, needing, trying and want, want, WANTING! Although these ways did produce results in the short term, giving the other children the Golden Tickets; they didn't get very good outcomes and certainly not the outcomes you would call magical or dreamy.

Charlie, some would say, was in the right place at the right time. I would say he followed the magic of life and that he was as happy as he could be, given his life situation. He appreciated everything he did have, whilst keeping his dreams alive, and even after the magic didn't happen, he still found magic in the little things and was grateful to be alive and have a family.

Charlie is connected with his Inner Spirit.

The Universe worked out all of the details for him; the Angels were singing along with him and even when Willy Wonka himself turned out to be a bit of a 'Wonka Plonka,' Charlie kept the faith.

Let's all be more Charlie; let's play this game of life and have some fun whilst doing it!

In this book, I share lots about playing and having fun in life, so I need to share more about the 'Game of Life' before I finish this chapter. When I say this, it always reminds me of a board game I used to play when I was a kid, and as the name suggests, it was a 'bored game' as well as being a traditional board-based game. It was called 'The Game of Life.' Do you remember it?

The aim of the game was to go around the board with a little plastic car within which there would be either a blue or pink peg that represented the person, colour-dependent upon whether you were a boy or a girl. On each spin of the number dial in the centre, you would move along and land on different squares as you wound around the snaky pathway. School, college and university came first, then onto landing on a job square with various wages and qualifications; then you would pass over a bridge at a certain point and get a husband or wife and kids at some point, adding more little pink and blue pegs to your car along the way. There were also holiday squares and other life experience squares you could land on if you were lucky enough.

Eventually you crossed over another bridge and reached retirement.

I can see why someone thought to create this game back in the eighties and I'm sure it would be a very different game now; maybe with a square to land on for when you get your first iPhone or join Facebook! I'd actually quite like to create a modern version of one, with a much more free-flowing and open view about life and how it should be; one where it was OK to have two pink or blue pegs in the front seats if that was your choice in life as well as pegs for dogs or cats rather than kids and maybe a square to land on saying 'adventures travelling the world' or maybe 'writing a book' or 'becoming an actor.' The options would be infinite, as they are in life, and maybe I would pop a few random squares in there, asking what it is that you feel you would love to do in life and encouraging you to do just that.

The reason I chose to share this particular example, is that the kind of 'Game of Life' that we choose to play is our own choice, which is driven by our belief systems; set out before us by the kind of upbringing we may have had or what people told us we should be doing when we were growing up, as well as by what society depicts.

Let's take a moment to Breathe, Relax and Allow any limiting beliefs which were given to us as children, or at any other times in our lives, to drift away. Things that we were told: that we were supposed to be a certain way and do certain things in life to be successful or have happy lives; go to school, get a good education, grow up and get a good job (or the best we can manage), get married, have a family, work hard, live for the weekends and holidays, grow old, retire and die.

I'm Sorry, I know that sounded a bit morbid, but for some this is true, but is it their truth or someone else's?

What if the Game of Life that we choose to play could be one of adventure, magic, enlightenment and wonderment?

Similar to the movie of life we are choosing to write our own scripts for, we can choose what Games of Life we are playing and program life in the way that we choose.

Look at computer games that have different levels. When you have completed a task or collected some kinds of coins or treasures from one level, you can then move to the next. I'm not saying that it's wrong, or not good to be a certain way or on a particular life level, as we are all on our own unique journeys, but what if we could view it in this way to simply see where we are at in life.

The life lessons we can learn from and sometimes endure; the obstacles which may appear in our way; the different decisions we make and the different paths we choose, along with the gems of knowledge we collect and learn from along the way.

If I hadn't played this game of life the way I have until this point, maybe I wouldn't be here writing this book. If you hadn't played it the way you have, maybe you wouldn't be here reading it or choosing to do the things you are now doing in life. The game can be played however we choose.

Maybe you like the thought of receiving different vibrational keys to open doors of opportunity. Maybe you can look at life's cycles a little like you are Lara Croft in Tomb Raider and have to go back to get another piece of the puzzle before you can move onto the next level - another piece of wisdom to give you your keys to the kingdom which represents your most magical life.

You decide which game you would like to play.

There are also the 'negative' or restrictive games we play, where something is hard or never seems to be working out. Perhaps just like those horrible shooting games, which I've never played myself, but of which I am aware; where there's worry about what we will be faced with around every corner and a need to watch our backs in case something bad happens. No thank you! Letting all of that one go!

I'd much rather be finding treasures and moving up life levels along the way, rather than being stuck in some fearful, dark, scary and bleak place, fearing every moment.

For me, the treasure game feels good and I hope it does to you too.

Chapter 16

Connecting With The Magic Of You ❤

YOUniverse

One of my fave non-word words.

This is your Magical YOUniverse and you are doing great!

When was the last time you looked in the mirror, smiled at yourself and said "You're Doing Great?"

When did you last wrap your arms around yourself and give yourself a great big hug?

Hugs are SO healing!

As human beings, in our imperfections (remember: imperfect = I'm~perfect), we often find it easier to put ourselves down, to beat ourselves up about what we aren't doing right, how we're not feeling the right way or looking at our flaws and not feeling good about ourselves. I know, I do it too - looking in the mirror and picking fault.

Looking at the things we think we've failed at in life or thinking that we haven't done what we should have or that we haven't created what we wanted. By doing this, we aren't connecting with our light within. That's why these kinds of feelings don't feel good, as we are disagreeing with our Inner Spirit, our truth and the Universal Truth that we are enough just as we are. Just like the practice we did in an earlier truth connecting chapter, when I told you that you were no good, useless and rubbish. Do you remember the feelings that brought up? Contractions as opposed to the feelings of me saying that you are a beautiful, light being with infinite possibilities and that you ARE good enough and that you are OK. YOU ARE MAGICAL.

In case there is any part of you that is saying "no" to this right now, or feeling that tightness around it; keep breathing as deeply as you can, breathe into it and let's set the intention for it to start to clear as you read this chapter.

A fabulous way to know how you are feeling about yourself is to look at the people around you; the mirrors of life.

I believe those around us reflect all of the different parts of ourselves. Ok, yes, it may be a part of us from years ago, from the past or even from past lives, but it's something which is still in our subconscious makeup, or even in our unconsciousness. This is a good get-out clause to release some of the resistance the mirror process can bring up and it can be quite intense.

Whatever is being mirrored back to us, even if it's an old part of us, must still be resonating in some way and on some level, otherwise we wouldn't attract it and we wouldn't be resonating with it. The same goes for the situations and circumstances which surround us, because mirroring goes for anything. Use it how you choose.

Start to notice who's around you. Who are you manifesting in your life?

What kind of people? What kind of lifestyle, situations and circumstances?

I know that it's easier sometimes to think about moving away from certain people, but I will say this; that they are there for a reason. Everything is showing up for a reason and the reflections they give us, allow us the opportunity to change from within; to clear our vibes and that part of us which still resonates with whoever or whatever it is. The trigger gives us the indicator that this is still here for us, and once we know it's here, we can then choose to clear.

As I mentioned earlier in the book (and a fab example of this), is a rubbish neighbour or boss. We want to move house or change our job and get a new one. I know, because I've done it myself.

Then we move or start a new job or business and the very same kind of person shows up. Sometimes, they even have a similar look to the last rubbish person or they have similar traits.

This happens in relationships too - new relationship, but similar person or problems showing up and people continually saying "Why do I keep attracting this kind of person????!!!"

How does this person reflect you? How does this situation or circumstance reflect you?

If it's not the kind of magic you would like reflecting back at you, then what's there to clear?

If you look back at your lifeline, or at least as far back as you can remember and connect with, how does this reflect the 'you' at that time in your life? What's similar? Why is it showing up again?

Another interesting thing is when people from your past pop back in; this can be both in your reality and in your dreams.

What's coming back in your vibration?

Maybe another life cycle to recycle?

Maybe some treasure that you forgot to collect on another life level?

Only you will know. Feel into it all. Really start to connect with and understand everything which is showing up around you.

It may not always feel like the treasures of life, but once cleared, life will become more magical.

This is the magic of what and who you are, vibrating and resonating with the world around you. Even if it doesn't feel good at the time, trust that it is as it's meant to be; an opportunity for change and growth and it's all good.

What I would love to talk about next is the magic of our bodies and how they function. I'm not going to go into too much detail, as I only really know the basics and may embarrass myself by not knowing the correct words and terminology. What I will say is this; I believe that our bodies are totally magical and often times, if we let go of trying to control too much, they heal naturally and continue to do every function required to give us spectacular body homes to live in.

This is leading me onto mentioning the magic of water and more importantly the water within us.

Have you heard about the amazing tests which were carried out in connection to vibes and water? I'm sure you have, but in case you haven't, look up Dr. Masaru Emoto. He passed into pure positive energy when he died in 2014, bless him. He was a great man who taught me a lot. To share just a little here today, the vibes we emit can affect the water around us, as well as the waters within us. To prove this, he sent different batches of water 'good' and 'bad' vibes. Peace, love, joy, hope, happiness and suchlike were sent to one and then anger, hate, stress, fear and suchlike to another. Dr. Emoto then froze the water and photographed the crystals and the results are amazing - take a look. The anger, hate stress and fear crystals are all jagged in shape. They look angry! The peace, love, joy, hope and happiness ones are like beautiful snowflakes and look magical.

I have also heard about Nikki Owen, who did a test on an apple by cutting it in half and putting it into two separate jam jars; sending one half the bad vibes and one half, the good stuff. What do you think happened? Give it a go for yourself. The apple which had been sent the bad vibes rotted really fast whereas the apple which was loved didn't rot anywhere near as quickly. This demonstrates what we are feeling and the vibes that we are emitting affects our bodies, which are mainly made up of water, as well as affecting the world around us which is filled with water.

Our bodies are affected by our vibes. Once again, it's all about balance here, as I know we can't always be filled with good vibes, up on high, all fine and dandy peeps all of the time, but we can identify the rotten vibes and with intention behind it, clear what's coming up and out; swiftly moving on and balancing harmony within our bodies. We can also send good vibes to that which we eat and drink; why do you think people pray to their food and say thank you before eating it?

It's not always possible for us to get hold of

organic, natural, home-grown produce, but we can improve the food which we do have and the same goes for the water that we drink. I use a filter jug so that it's clearer, but I also have a sticker on the bottom of it with the words love, peace, balance, joy, happiness, thank you, bliss, appreciation, gratitude and suchlike, as well as lots of sparkly love hearts stuck to it! We can change the vibration of that which we put into our bodies.

I have recently 'released' almost two stone by eating healthier foods and walking more. Plus, I dog walk for people in the village, so it's easy to be out there rambling through the fresh air in the local countryside, breathing in life.

I have always walked quite a lot and didn't really eat massively unhealthily, but as you already know, I do like my wine. That said, I do my best to let my body cleanse the toxins naturally. I believe in practical steps alongside the 'Invisible Spiritual Steps.' Again, it's about balance.

I took inspired action and started a new, healthy eating regime, yet I still allow myself to have what might be labelled as not-so-good foods and drinks in moderation (usually, lol!). Whatever I am eating, I make sure that I am enjoying it. Great example... this afternoon, in-between my typing, we've been for a blustery walk over the hills. I decided I was going to treat myself to a cream scone and really enjoy it. It was cherry and almond, homemade at our local farm, and it was delicious. I sent it love and good vibes and really enjoyed every last crumb of it, trusting my body to dispose of that which it doesn't need.

I also have to add here a few years ago, I did try my own version of vibrational dieting; 'try' being the operative word. I was eating whatever I fancied and trying to send it good vibes, but at the same time, I was feeling really shit for eating too much of the wrong kind of food; foods which I knew didn't serve me in big quantities. So the vibes weren't really good; it didn't feel balanced and I gained weight both physically and vibrationally!

I feel a little treat every now and again does us the world of good. Whatever your vice is, be it chocolate cake, cheese and wine, or cream scones; start to allow yourself to feel ok with that and when you do feel ok with that, then you can treat yourself. If you are feeling bad, then don't have it; and if you are feeling bad and do have it, forgive yourself and move on. Go for a walk or do something different to take your mind off it and release any resistance you have.

I used to be a secret cheese eater as a kid: 'Lizzy Mouse!' I had a real love-hate relationship with eating cheese. I got chubbier and chubbier and my feelings got worse and worse - a cycle of not-so-Magical Manifesting. I feel much easier about food now, eating more than I ever used to when I was dieting. Btw, what do you get if you take the letter 'T' off the word diet? That's right! DIE. When we go on faddy diets, our bodies think we are going to die and start to store fat up, meaning we just end up putting weight back on. A healthier daily regime for life, I feel, is much better. For me, I love being part of a community, so I decided to go back to Weight Watchers and have manifested an amazing, supportive leader and lovely group of people and we all cheer each other along.

This way, I can also let myself have whatever I fancy when on holiday or away for the weekend. We've been eating lots of lovely food here in Spain, although I did say to my chap last night that I was feeling a little heavy and bloated, so we have been light about food today and eaten lots of healthy things. The heavy bloating feelings let us know we need to lighten up. Our bodies always let us know; it either feels light and bright or heavy and dark.

One of the other 'magics' of you I would like to share more about, is your magical flow and what you love to do.

Are you a creative type who loves to paint and make things?

Do you love to talk, write or share words?

Do you love helping people? Making stuff? Sharing stuff?

Maybe you love animals or travel?

What sets your heart on fire?

What would you love to be doing in life?

Wouldn't it be wonderful to spring out of bed each morning excited about the day ahead? I feel like that most days now, but I haven't always.

I used to say that I wasn't a morning person and didn't function very well until after lunchtime. I was creating that in my reality by saying it, and at the time, I really didn't enjoy what I was doing for the majority of the week - in particular Monday through Friday!

When we are connecting with our magical path and the magic of who we really are, mixed with what we really love to do as much of the time as possible, then life is really exciting and in flow. We are excited about each new day and what it brings. Contractive non-magical thoughts and feelings, such as worries, constrict this flow and I know that all too well. Do you?

I also know that we can be following the magic of who we really are and what we really love to do and then sabotage it with our self-doubts and worries, which once again stop the flow and can also stop us in our tracks. This is a cycle I have been through in the past and one which I have been revisiting again as I share this book. I have cleared and am clearing this as much as I can. As I mentioned earlier in the book, my chap and me are going through a tough time right now and it can become consuming; meaning that I stop my inspired flow and become like a rabbit in the headlights, scared and not knowing what to do, then not doing anything at all.

Have you ever felt like that?

The redundancy for my chap was voluntary

and absolutely meant to be. It was Magical Manifesting, and even though many may not think redundancy is magical, in this case it was. He'd worked for the company for twenty four long years and was just about ready to walk out of the door anyway, so he manifested a better situation out of a not-so-ideal situation and at least he got some redundancy money. I used to work at the same company too, so I could see this particular cycle replaying, as well as appreciating cutting the ties with the said company, which was no longer a great place to work. When he left, it felt like a big grey cloud had been removed from over our lives together.

Since leaving, he has manifested some amazing opportunities to support him to be his own boss and to follow his heart. As I have mentioned, it's also bringing up some of my old fears and concerns, and a part of me still wanted to cloud the excitement with the 'what ifs?' What if this doesn't happen? What if that doesn't happen? What if we run out of money and lose everything? What if? What if? What if?

Have you ever felt like this?

Clearing all of all of that, thank you very

muchly! It's time to be free of these 'worry beans' and to enjoy each moment and each day again, and, as I sit and type this here today, I feel that lightness; the lightness of following the magic of me and sharing these stories with you all. What a gift! Thank you, thank you, thank you!

I am going to practice more of what I preach and clear these worry beans once and for all, if that is at all possible! I know in my heart of hearts that this Universe has got our backs and that all will be well. Everything is just as it's meant to be and in Divine Order and that goes for all of us.

I know from past experiences that if I let the worry bean part of me take over without clearing up on where it's coming from, then it will stop me in my tracks and I really feel there ain't no stopping me now! Sing it with me!

"Ain't no stopping us now, we're on the move! Ain't no stopping us now, we're in the groove!"

Clearing up on what's ready to go and allowing the magical flow. The intention is set!

If you have gone through, or are going through, anything similar in your life, let's clear it for you too. The intentions are set and the magical balls (oooo errrr mrs! lol) are rolling!

Can you feel it?

Going back to the story, my chap and me have been totally freed up to do what we love and to follow our hearts. Don't get me wrong, we have done some upstream paddling and had lots of ups and downs, as we all do in life, but we are open to divine guidance and following the energy as it flows. I wonder what the magical possibilities are for us both now?

Here in Spain, we took a beautiful walk around the castle and the archaeological sites this morning and I breathed deeply, feeling the energy of all of the history and all of those years of evolution and growth. I felt the comfort of knowing that we are all totally supported every step of the way and that all will be well. After seeing the historical sites and lots of cute Spanish kitty cats along the way, we chose to have lunch in a lovely bustling square nearby, with the church bells ringing and with us chilling and relaxing.

Whilst in Spain, I've been continually seeing signs (actual signs! lol!) for Flamenco dance evenings. I would have loved to have seen the Flamenco dancers, but a full evening of it didn't really appeal to me. As we sat at our table, a lady walked passed me dressed in Flamenco dress, carrying a wooden board, as she set out her stall to dance and entertain us all with some beautiful dancing just across from where we were sitting. She was superbly confident and in flow, as well as being powerfully 'in the moment,' as she tapped and danced to her very own unique rhythm and to everyone's delight. I feel this is the perfect example, given to me to include in this chapter about getting in touch with our magic; being in flow and most importantly being confident about who we really are and sharing our unique gifts, talents and abilities with the world.

What's your 'Magical Dance' of life?

What areas of you and your life have you pushed away?

Have you pushed away your confidence in exchange for insecurities, worries, fears and self judgements or maybe you've allowed what others may think or say about you to stop you in your tracks.

I did it for nearly six years, saying I was going to write books. I would start and stop and never quite get there, feeling I wasn't good enough or doubting if what I had to share was worthwhile sharing.

Now I feel I have reached a point where it was hurting too much not to do it. I had an ache; a feeling something was missing if I didn't write and share what I have to share. It actually hurts to think about not doing this and it also hurts when I think about doing things that I don't want to do anymore.

Do you know what I mean?

If you think about something you would love to do, or know you should be doing a certain thing, then you have some purpose you would love to fulfil in your Magical YOUniverse.

What would that be?

What does it hurt to think about not doing in your life?

What calling do you have which can no longer be ignored and if you did ignore it and leave this planet without fulfilling it, how would that feel?

Ouch. Can you feel that?

It's time to follow our callings and to trust the process, to tune into our heart path and walk boldly along it.

Are you with me? Let's do it!

I will vibrationally hold your hand as you do, as you are for me, reading these words, and let's trust that it's all totally worth it.

The one thing I have realised along the way is that we need to stop beating ourselves up for not doing the stuff we know or feel we should be doing in life, and to trust it will happen when the timing is right too. I know there are so many factors involved. We are surfing the wave of life, but sometimes the waves aren't quite right or ready to jump on and ride and other times we jump on in and fall off our vibrational surf boards and that's ok too.

Confidence comes with experience and each moment that we live is a part of that experience.

Let me share one of my favourite passages with you here today. When I volunteered on the local radio show, I managed to find an excuse to share this particular passage a few times, as well as sharing at workshops in the past and I always get covered in Godbumps every time I share. You will probably also notice that I have quoted other writers or used quotes from others in this book. Although I have probably shared a lot, I have learnt from other people and books that I have read and put this into my own words and that's how life flows; we are all here to learn from each other and thank you to everyone who so kindly shared their vibes with me - it's much appreciated.

Anyway, I will stop judging my writing abilities now and share the passage. You will love it, of that I am certain.

The passage 'Our Deepest Fear" is by Marianne Williamson and it is taken from a book called 'Return to Love.'

Our Deepest Fear ~

"Our deepest fear is not that we are inadequate. Our deepest fear is that we are powerful beyond measure. It is our light, not our darkness that most frightens us.

We ask ourselves, who am I to be brilliant, gorgeous, talented, fabulous?

Actually, who are you not to be? You are a child of God.

Your playing small does not serve the world. There is nothing enlightened about shrinking so that other people won't feel insecure around you. We are all meant to shine, as children do. We were born to make manifest the glory of God that is within us.

It's not just in some of us; it's in everyone. And as we let our own light shine,

we unconsciously give other people permission to do the same. As we are liberated from our own fear, our presence automatically liberates others."

—Marianne Williamson

It's our time to SHINE!

Can you feel that truth?

Chapter 17

The Magic of Connection ♥

As cheesy as it sounds, we are all one, we are all connected, and most importantly, we are all in this thing called life together, alongside this magnificent Universe. It's time to plug in and get connected.

The times when I experience lots of magical things in life, are the times when I've been taking inspired (In~Spirit) action. Ok, I know I've already shared with you that maybe I used to take a little or a lot of the action-based stuff first (and maybe it wasn't always inspired), but we learn as we go along. Now, I feel I am much more in balance with all of this.

During times of movement in my life, lots of synchronicities start to happen and I feel really connected and plugged in. I know I've mentioned this earlier in the book, but I feel it's a good time for a reminder here again about the goosebumps or 'Godbump' tingles and energy flowing, which happen when we are following our truth and moving along with it. It's a case of getting out there in the world, connecting with and meeting people, sharing and co-creating together, whilst being as upbeat as we can about what we are doing in our lives right now. This also inspires others and things start to flow as if by magic!

On a side note, I have to slip in here having shared what I have about how life is unfolding around me, the magic IS happening. Over these last few days, lots of things which felt 'stuck' in our lives have now started to flow. Projects which were started months ago and which weren't quite 'happening' are now happening and I have nearly finished this book too. It's all totally aligned and maybe all of those hours of worrying that I had decided to do, over the past however many months, just weren't necessary. That said, at times, that was how I felt and I had to honour that. I just wanted to let you know that the things which are meant to happen in life will; when we are making moves and living the lives we are here to live, no matter what. It feels really good to share this with you, as I really didn't, and really still don't, know what will happen in life; but I am keeping the faith and feeling hopeful, hope is a very good place to be.

My fave quote, which I shared at the end of the last chapter, came to me in a book I was given whilst I was running 'Magical Meet Ups' a number of years ago. I set these get-togethers up after I completed my Law of Attraction Facilitator training back in 2011.

I would simply go out and meet like-minded people and chat about what magic we were creating in our lives at the time, and the kind of magical things we would like to manifest in the future, as well as showing gratitude for the 'now' moment. I met so many amazing friends and made great connections by doing this.

I love to blog and make YouTube videos and this has also been a wonderful way to connect and meet people. As an example, my friend who I attended the Sweat Lodge with, which I shared more about earlier met me through YouTube a few years back. She was watching one of my videos and noticed I had a similar accent to her and thought I must be local - which I was - and we met up for a lovely walk and now have a great friendship to share. How cool is that? We are all so connected in so many different ways and when we plug into this and take inspired action, who knows what it will lead to?

As we know, there are no coincidences in life - just incidences that perfectly coincide.

All this as well as being an energetic way to plug into and connect with Magical Manifesting. It always seems what I say on videos and the intentions I set, eventually come to fruition; well, they do when I'm not interfering and worrying about making it happen. In my moments of letting go, I see the magic flow. Funny that, isn't it?

I have just posted a picture on Facebook of my cat, Levi, sat on my writing book. He's decided to come and help me to type the book up on this wild and blustery, rainy afternoon, curled up next to the warmth of the radiator, listening to Enya with me. As I share this, he's reminding me of the magic of YouTube, which got my cats, Levi and Lloyd, a Saturday night prime time spot on TV. When they were a few years old – they are six now – my chap and me made a silly video of them dancing to a rap song. They were perfectly in time to the music and kept putting their paws in the air in time to the music. I think the name of the video on YouTube is 'Gangster Rapping Kittens Levi and Lloyd.' From the said video, I was contacted by a TV programme called *Animal Antics* to ask if they could use the footage. A few months later, there they were, dancing on the TV and all because I love sharing things on YouTube! Look at the opportunity it led to.

YouTube is also the way in which I meet and connect with many of my coaching clients and it's wonderful, as they feel like they already know me and my cups of tea! I am very grateful for this way of connecting and sharing and I am also wondering what other amazing opportunities it can lead to?

I've always fancied myself being on the telly again. One of my claims to fame is being in a couple of episodes of the famous Yorkshire based TV show 'Last of the Summer Wine.' I loved it! I also now live nearby to where this was filmed. I would definitely be open to more work on TV. What an amazing way to connect with lots of people at once, and we could definitely do with more inspiring and uplifting TV programmes.

What do you think?

I can remember as far back as being a small child that I have always loved connecting with people, and that I have always loved to chat to people to share more about me, who I was and what I was up to. My mum used to call me the little sunshine girl, smiling at everyone, chatting and connecting. I'm not sure she was always that impressed with my openness when I was at the bus stop, telling everyone how old she was, but I'm sure it was still cute!

It's time to lift our heads up high, to get out there in the world, meet new people and allow the sunshine to beam from our hearts. Ironic that it's so stormy outside! I do remember the sun shining in Spain whilst I was writing this book though, and it's lovely to be able to add to it and share more and more magic. All in Divine Order. It's time for us all to connect more and more, whether that is online or offline. I must say that connecting in person is much better, but sometimes an online connection leads to more, as it has in my life.

I met up with another like-minded spreader of positive vibes who was sharing her journey on YouTube. We decided to meet up in person and the energy was amazing; a lady in the town where we met must have sensed our vibes and asked how we knew each other; she didn't even know what YouTube was and didn't really do the World Wide Web. She decided that we were like pen pals who had met up for the very first time and that's exactly what it felt like - unions of souls who are meant to be together. Your vibe attracts your tribe and our tribes are coming back together in a whole new and modern way. I feel as though I am a part of lots of different tribes in lots of different ways and I appreciate very much how we have all come together.

How about you?

Are you joining with your tribes?

I would like to share a lovely story here about the power of connection, heart to heart. ❤

Around five years ago, I decided to do a free hugs event. At the time, as you know, I was going through some other big life changes, and vibrational changes, as well as emotional, shifts. Hugs are very healing, so I decided to arrange a Magical Meet-Up in our local city, which is called Wakefield and I called it 'Awakeningfield,' lol! We made some Cardboard Cutout free hugs signs in a café next to the cathedral, whilst our excitement and nerves were building. Questions kept running through my mind, such as, who would we be hugging? Would people join in? Would we look silly?

We may have looked a little silly, but people did join in! People loved it! We had a busker playing his tunes next to us and faces started to light up as we held up our boards with open arms and open hearts. It was totally magical and very,

very connected. I tingled with goosebumps the whole day through!

Around halfway through the day, a gorgeous little old chap came along and started taking photos of us on his old 1970's style camera, which he had around his neck. Clicking away as his smile grew wider and wider, I called him closer to come and get a hug, he shook his head and pointed at his camera, saying "it's ok, I'm just taking pictures."

On another little side note here, I am reminded that the morning I wrote this in Spain, during our visit to the historical sites, both my chap and me realised we had forgotten our phones, which we normally take photos on. I said that was cool, as sometimes, we can end up looking at life through a lens and it's much better to be present in the moment if we can, without the lens, as well as taking photos if that's what we choose. Again, it's about balance. I definitely took more in and really 'felt' into my surroundings, making mental pictures.

With such things as 3G and 4G and whatever other online connectivity we have, it can sometimes be all-consuming and we can miss what is happening around us. With everything at the click of a button, we can sometimes get lost in it and miss the 'now' moments - becoming that connected online, we can end up somewhat disconnected from life. Again, it's about finding our own healthy balance with this modern way of living. Ha ha! I sound like I'm about ninety, don't I?

So... yes, back to the old chap with the camera who just wanted to take pictures. I asked him again to "come and have a hug, you can take more pictures afterwards!" I reached out to him and he reached back and we shared a warm and beautiful hug. I sensed it was pulling on his heartstrings, and as I looked at him, I saw that he was crying and that his face was covered in tears. He whispered to me that his wife had died two years earlier and he thought he would never have another hug. That was, he said "until today, thank you so much!" That set me off blubbering and I waved over my fellow huggers, shouting out "group hug required over here ladies!" We just hugged and hugged and hugged him, tears flowing freely, and people just stood and watched and smiled on. He walked away absolutely beaming from ear to ear. Pure divine connection - that's for sure! And how wonderful that he got this magical connection, as well as his photos to remember it by!

Writing about this and sharing it with you has made me cry again and I've got sun cream in my eyes now too and they are streaming. In contrast, back here in rainy old England, I am letting Mother Nature do the crying for me with her torrential rain!

When we open to the magic of connection and life and all of its amazing wonders, the tears do flow and they can flow a lot; and that's ok too. Let them flow freely. They wash our eyeballs so that we can see more clearly. They clear the sun cream, or should that be 'the sunscreen,' from our eyes, so we can see much more clearly and connect with the light, the inner and outer sunshine which is always beaming - even if it's behind the clouds. These kinds of connection are divinely orchestrated and are given to us each and every day - if we choose to connect to them, that is. You don't need to go and do free hugs events, although if you do, it's a wonderful gift to give and I would highly recommend it.

This everyday magic is right here, right now and we can choose to connect with it in each and every moment.

Take a look around you, wherever you are

right now, and breathe deeply and just feel the magic around you, connect and plug in.

I am reminded of another film connection here. Have you seen the film *Love Actually?* There is an airport scene, where everyone's connecting, hugging each other, kissing and smiling or even crying as their loved ones return home or embark on a trip away or maybe even a brand new life journey. We fly home tomorrow and I intend to connect with this energy. I always have this intention as much as I can, wherever I am going and whatever I am doing; to connect deeply with people and be open.

I feel I also want to share here about the sensitivity of being aware and awakening to this way of being. I have read other teachings about protecting ourselves and our energy from others or from certain situations. Empaths, who feel a lot, and I do get where these teachings are coming from, as I am very empathic and I know it can get intense and be overwhelming.

Sometimes, visiting busy, bustling places can feel off-balance for me, like today, when we were in the café which I mentioned earlier. I had been very tuned in to the history and energy of the castle and my vibes felt very open. When we reached the square, there were lots of people around and lots of different vibes, as well as the different vibes of the places around us. I started to feel a little off-balance, so I breathed deeply, silently asking that whatever was coming up to make me feel this way, would clear. I asked for it to clear so I could feel more balanced and comfortable and enjoy this experience. I did this rather than 'closing-off,' blocking anything, or having to 'bubble' myself.

I believe that if we feel we need to protect ourselves from certain energies and vibes, we will attract more of the said things we are fearful about and require more protection. I know this to be true for me, as I feel it helped towards manifesting dis...ease in my life, as well as more worry. I understand that it's good to be conscious about how we are feeling and what will serve us best at each point of our lives and that's cool. I also feel that we can choose to cherry-pick what we are taking part in or being a part of in life, and if we do feel we require spiritual support to help strengthen us up, such as a Golden Light or Angels around us then that's cool too. I feel it's good to be more aware of when or why we are doing this.

From my own experience, it's good to let stuff come knocking at our door, clear up the feelings it's bringing, and then make the choice to let it in or not - and usually by simply clearing up the feelings, the knocking will stop. The resistance to whatever it is goes away and with the lack of resistance comes the flow and the letting go, and guess what, it goes!

I feel life is here to be lived, to say "yes" to, hopefully without being too afraid to say "yes" and to accept what that "yes" may bring into our lives; to powerfully trust that we are supported every step of the way, whether we are sat in a busy café, or stood on a stage in front of hundreds or even thousands of people. Yes, its ok to say no too when certain people, places or experiences don't feel right for us and only we will know this for ourselves.

Once again, there is a balanced way for each of us to connect with; we are all totally unique and so we have to follow what feels right to us in each life experience. One thing I will say is this; if we are bubbling ourselves off, maybe our connection just can't quite connect.

What do you feel?

What if the more we clear and cleanse our vibes and become the best possible versions of ourselves in each moment, then we will receive 'Universal Hugs' of magical alignment where everything is ok; and by simply breathing, relaxing and allowing that, that is enough. That feels good now, doesn't it?

Nice and easy.

Nice and flowing.

Open and trusting.

Releasing the resistance.

Chapter 18

Divine Magic ❤

I saved this last chapter to write whilst on the flight home, once again trusting the process that all is in Divine Order; plus my aching fingers wanted a rest! I'm glad I waited, and knew this was the right timing, as so many signs have been sent my way; one really funny one in particular which was much to the amusement of my chap.

I often ask the Angels to support me, so this morning we were up bright and early and I was setting the intention that we would have a safe and hopefully, magical journey home. All was well. The Angels travelled with us and I was really feeling the divine connection. When we arrived to drop Betty, the hire car (the thinking person's car) off, we parked in bay eleven on the first floor. There were 111's everywhere, letting us know that we were embarking on new paths; we were checking in at gate 222; with the 2's letting us know that we are on the right path and to keep going. Our brunch and drinks at the airport lounge even came to 22.20 Euros and we were sitting in seats 11A and 11B for the flight home.

I knew that Divine Order was at work and letting us know all was well, even though a little part of me felt some sadness to be leaving such a beautiful, warm place, as well as coming home to the unknown of our situation and where we would be led. That said, I did have lots of excitement bubbling up about getting home and typing up this book, as well as seeing our fur family and the beautiful countryside around our cottage. I felt ready for getting back into everyday life and ready for lots of lovely walks and more refreshing, fresh cool air (which is actually freezing air at the moment, with a chance of snow at the weekend!). Since returning home we've had mini-hurricanes and it's been wild winds and rain, with the sun peeping through to shine upon lots of magical rainbows, which seemed to be everywhere I went on my dog walks. Great signs!

Back to the flight... I haven't always been a nervous traveller, but I do tend to tense up and want to rush around when there are schedules to meet, such as take-off times. There is also a part of me that doesn't like not being in control. Do you ever feel that? Let's clear this and let go more and more.

As we now know, the more we try to control anything, the more control will be needed, which, I feel, causes unnecessary tensions and stresses. It's time to let go and fly freely! Weeeeeeeeeeeeee! Off we go!

The pilot's taking care of the details for the next few hours; just like the Universe takes care of the details when we ask. This Magical Universe will always step in and support us on our life journeys, including today and the here and now.

Anyway, I digress. The funny thing which happened was that I kept chatting to my chap about all the synchro's, magic and flow and how I was so pleased I had a window seat. On the flight out, we didn't have window seats to start with and this made me feel a little anxious; yes, it was good stuff to clear what was making me feel this way, but I still wanted a nice view from the window. The lady next to me on the flight out must have been tuning into my vibes, as she moved seats once we had taken off, which allowed me to slide over into the seat I desired and appreciate the stunning view over the clouds and the sun setting.

So on the way home, I was well chuffed that we had the perfect seats and I could look out of the window and connect with divine energy and enjoy the angelic looking clouds whilst writing about divine connection. Or so I thought!

It turned out that I had manifested the only non-window seat on my side of the plane. As I shuffled into my seat, I could hear my chap chuckling behind me as he joked that I had manifested this outcome with all of the moaning I had done on the way there. Oops! Me, moaning! Never! lol!

It was so funny! I was a little pissed off, but couldn't help but laugh and if I leaned right back to the window behind me, I had a tiny, little strip of a viewpoint over my shoulder. Maybe from now on, I will always have a fabulous window seat with wonderful views... or maybe not... It's all good!

Putting into practice what I have shared in this book, I changed my feelings of disappointment about the non-window seat and swiftly moved onwards and upwards, knowing that if this hadn't have happened, I wouldn't be sharing this example here today; the perfect example of Divine Magic - even when it doesn't really feel divine and we don't get what we think we want. You see, as I don't have a window to stare out of and get lost in the lovely views, I know I will focus more on these writings, which are also helping me to feel really grounded. Maybe if this hadn't happened, I wouldn't have ended up finishing this last chapter. I know divine energy is still with you, and me, and it matters not where we are or what we can see.

As I keep saying, it's all good and is always in total Divine Order. Can you tell this is one of my favourite sayings?

Now that there are no distractions for me; write I will!

I am sure you will have heard stories about people going 'what they thought' was the wrong way, or being late when driving somewhere and missing an accident. I know the late thing is a bit of a contradiction, when actually we are always on time anyway, as there is no time, but we do have practical life things to take care of too. So let's just say we are always right where we are supposed to be, and when we can trust, this life flows, as does the Divine Order of which I speak so much.

Start to look at things differently and speak about things differently. Rather than apologising for being late, or taking wrong turns - both practically and in life - simply say "it's all in Divine Order; I'm right where I am meant to be at this particular time" and the same goes for our lives; those twists and turns, ups and downs and round and arounds; we are being guided along the way and moving through the contrasts of what we don't desire, to reach the clarity of what we do desire and we are clearing up along the way to reach a life that we truly love.

Divine/dɪˈvʌɪn

adjective 1.

of or like God or a god. 'heroes with divine powers'

informal

very pleasing; delightful.

I feel that each and every one of us is the 'God Energy' that so many people seek outside of themselves. We are the heroes with the divine power and it is delightful.

I did a coaching session recently with a lovely lady and we talked about super powers. She is becoming a coach and we chatted about how life is all of the experience we require. Life is our teacher. That, alongside all of our unique gifts and talents, creates divinely connected magic.

So for example, I would say my 'Superpower' is my ability to be very sensitive to what others are feeling, as well as visually tuning in to what they share with me. I can put myself in their shoes and offer back to them a fresh perspective and 'take' on things, which brings wonderful clarity; this, as well as feeling and knowing when people need help or support, or maybe even just a smile or a hug, which I always offer freely, and my way with words and how to share them. I like to think of myself as a 'Word Artist.'

Play along with me.

What's your Superpower?

How can you inspire and delight yourself and others?

What does 'Divine' mean to you and how do you connect with this energy?

Some people connect via praying or meditating, or, like me, by synchro and 'sign' spotting; maybe through yoga, 'Conscious Connected Breathing,' attending church or spiritual groups, or simply by walking in nature, taking a nap or just being present. I feel there really is no right or wrong way to connect with the divine and it matters not what you call it.

Can you feel the truth in this?

Each to their own and you will have your very own unique ways too. And for any part of us who wants to control how others connect with 'Divine,' maybe it's time to let that go too, letting go of any preaching.

I'm laughing to myself as I type these words, as I know that I am a great preacher and have done lots of preaching in my life. As a child, when I used to go knocking on doors, and then again as an adult, spreading my positive vibes and being a pioneer of positive change.

Knock, knock, knock!

Now, I prefer to take a more relaxed and natural approach as much is possible; to be a 'Lighthouse;' rather than swimming out or rowing out to others in distress, to simply shine a light and allow them to come if they are connecting with the light. This to me feels divine.

For me, naturally sharing and co-creating with each other, as each of us follows our own truths, feels much more magical, and this, in turn, creates the incidences that perfectly coincide, whereas from my own experiences, the preaching to others of the 'right' and 'wrong' ways can often feel heavy and closed off. It's time to wake up and know that each and every one of us has our own Divine Truth from within.

SHIT! Do I sound like I'm preaching now?!?!? Oh well, it's all good! lol

It's all in Divine Order. Hey! I did say I am taking a more relaxed approach as much as I can and that I am doing my best, as you are, so that's ok. You are doing your best with where you are and with what you have learnt in life so far. Let's be easy on ourselves. We are each on different life journeys and at different stages and we each know our own truths. This was why I felt guided to share the chapters about connecting with your own truth earlier in this book, so you can make up your own minds and hearts on the matter. I feel that this was a good 'former preacher' get out clause, lol!

What feels like your truth about 'Divine?'

What do you call 'Divine' in your life and how do you magically connect with this energy for love and support?

Go with that and trust your feelings, and if it's totally different to lots of other people's belief systems and opinions, that's cool too; be ok with this.

Just because we are on a Spiritual Journey, this doesn't mean that we all have to do things in a certain way. For example, I don't meditate, although I do enjoy my weekly yoga class. I prefer to get creative and make jewellery, including gratitude bracelets, as well as walking in nature and connecting with what is 'My Divine.' I have also recently acquired a Shamanic Drum, so I'm drumming myself home, back to the heart of me and of who I really am.

Or if I'm on a plane flying through the air, I decide I am going to see Angel Clouds in the sky; to me that's divine. Or maybe I will just be faced with a wall and no window. Going back to this, I really feel it holds symbolic meaning for me right now and maybe this meaning is for you too.

Even though I may not be able see the expansive views ahead of me right now, except by contorting my body and being uncomfortable, the expansive views and visions will come back; the views will return. I've been so laser-focused on sharing these words during the last week or so, that maybe I haven't been as caught up in what's happening around me so much, but more with what's been coming from within.

Do you know what I mean?

In conclusion, I would like to say "thank you 'Divine,' thank you Angels, God Source Energy, Great Spirit; thank you for guiding me and supporting me in this way. I feel you!"

Do you feel it too?

Goosebumps! Tingles! Ohhh WoW! I hope you can feel it too.

Close your eyes and take a

n i c e   d e e p   b r e a t h...
Ahhhhhhhhh...

that's it...

B r e a t h e   R e l a x   A l l o w

I feel life is opening up in a whole new direction. New opportunities are flowing in and new possibilities taking shape.

What new 'flow' are you inspired to follow, knowing all that you now know and have already known your whole life?

This book has just been a re~minder, a re~connection to who you really are.

You are a divine being, we all are.

Just like so much else that comes from within us, so does our light and it can literally light up the whole world if we allow it to.

No more shrinking violets and no more playing small or limiting ourselves.

It's our time to Shine and Shine brightly we will!

I believe that we have all travelled many lifetimes and learnt many lessons, and now, we have reached the time in life to become this energy of the totality of ourselves in all of our greatness. It's time for us to create change in the world, melding and moulding life as we evolve; taking inspired action and following our dreams. Even if our dreams feel out of reach right now, or maybe they feel a little weird or crazy. Crazy is good and this feels like the perfect time to share wonderful words from the late and great Steve Jobs... I also have to add here that from Googling this to share it here today, it appears it was actually written over one hundred years ago - not sure by whom first of all, but what I am sure of, is that it's fab and I love the freedom that it gives us to be our crazy selves!

"Here's to the crazy ones.

The misfits. The rebels. The troublemakers. The round pegs in the square holes.

The ones who see things differently. They're not fond of rules.

And they have no respect for the status quo.

You can praise them, disagree with them, quote them, disbelieve them, glorify or vilify them.

About the only thing you can't do is ignore them.

Because they change things. They invent. They imagine.

They heal. They explore. They create.

They inspire.

They push the human race forward. Maybe they have to be crazy.

How else can you stare at an empty canvas and see a work of art?

Or sit in silence and hear a song that's never been written?

Or gaze at a red planet and see a

laboratory on wheels?

While some may see them as the crazy ones, we see genius.

Because the people who are crazy enough to think they can change the world,

are the ones who do..."

- Steve Jobs

I guess that's why I call the world I live in 'Liz~Land.' It's mine to create and maybe no one else will ever quite get it, or maybe they will. What's your 'xxxx~Land?' Give it a name and let the magic flow. It can be as magical (or not-so-magical) as 'Liz~Land' if you choose for it to be so, and that includes everything; the good, the bad and the ugly, whatever it is to be, you deicide. And remember...

It's not about what you are experiencing in your life. It's how you feeeeeel about it.

Conclusion

The Magic Isn't Always Easy ❤

It's been just over seven months since we were last in Spain and I finished writing this book. I genuinely thought it would be out in the world by now and lots of lovely people (like your good self) would be reading it. Sometimes in life things take a lot longer than we first imagine and there are lots of road blocks along the way as well as changes to the original path we thought we would walk along.

During the last seven months a lot of contrast has come up to clear. Some of which I have shared here in this book, some of which has come up since the first draft was ready to re-read. This contrast has literally stopped me in my tracks at some points and it's what brought me back here to Spain today.

A lot of the contrast has been connected with my health challenges (challenges = opportunity to grow and hopefully eventually glow). It's my chap's birthday this week and, due to what some would say were stressful situations we have been through, his dear friend has gifted us this trip away here at his magical apartment in Almunecar, on the beach. I was ready for a break and some healing time, last week I didn't even know if we would make it here due to the Menieres Dis....ease popping back in to say hello again but I came up with a healing plan and I've made it here! Whoohoooo!

It's beautiful, warm and sunny and I am feeling better day by day. I already know my next book will be specifically about my journey with this particular dis....ease I've manifested in my life. *'Mastering Menieres the Magical Way'*

I know, I know, I haven't even finished this one yet – but by the time you are reading this I will have. Phew! All in divine timing and I am trusting the process. It's time for me to powerfully practice what I preach.

So yes, not everything has gone to plan, the way I'd planned it that is, yet I know in my heart it's the divine plan even though life has become even more difficult and uncertain. That said, I'm still here and I'm alive! In this now moment I'm happy and feeling really rather abundant. LG = Life's Good!

I feel that when we start to radically shift things in our lives and start following our true heart path we are breaking through what may be our own personal patterns and safety boundaries which we have put in place. This is often outside our comfort zone and outside our comfort zone is where the magic happens.

It's at this point that we discover that the magic isn't always easy. But this my dear friends, is the most important time to keep going. To keep moving towards our dreams and that which we most desire. That which keeps pulling us in the right direction. During the breakdowns we are then given the opportunity to rebuild our lives and clear up on the contrast and cycles we are manifesting.

I'm not saying this is how it happens to everyone so don't let this put you off. If you are up for manifesting the magic in your life and start putting into practice that which I have shared in this book just know that it may not always feel magical or be easy but I can promise you this.... It's worth it!

Following your heart and soul and committing to your own personal journey of truth and connecting with everyday magic is the best thing you will ever choose to do.

What if you decided not to do this and all the shit still hit the fan anyway?

We may as well go for it! What do you feel?

It's time to reach for the stars and follow your heart. ♥

Btw, I can't help giving myself one (or maybe two) last digressions and finishing on some little side notes. We've been back home for three weeks now and the final checks of the book are complete, the beautiful artwork for the cover is ready and lots of cool things are coming back into my life.

I went Firewalking again the other evening and have booked on a wonderful breathing weekend for in a month or so. It all feels really magical and aligned. It was during a Firewalk a few years back I set the intention to write a book so to find myself back in the same place intending to bring this, my first book, to completion was just perfect!

I made a pinky promise with a lovely new friend, who supported me to uncover the final blocks to getting this 'out there' in the world so here we go! Pinky promise achieved and there ain't no stopping me now!!

The most interesting thing which manifested at the event was my failed attempt at bending the rebar for the second time in my life (if you remember the first time was over in Mexico with my chap which I shared earlier). This time around I was trying far too hard and wanting and needing the bar to bend and it simply wouldn't budge. I've ended up with a huge bruise on my throat and a fabulous lesson to learn from this failure.

Failure/feɪljə/
Noun
1. lack of success.

2. the neglect or omission of expected or required action.

Did I have a lack of success?

Yes, but only in this one area and from this 'lack' a huge amount of vibrational clarity flowed about letting go of the needing, wanting and trying, so on second thoughts maybe this was a success!?!?! I believe it was.

Did I neglect the required action? No I took the leap and gave it a go. I took the inspired action and followed the urge to give it a go.

That's what I am going to invite you to do in your life. Take the leaps of faith and give things a go, whatever you have been wishing for, dreaming of and hoping would happen. I wish you the very best of success!

In case you were wondering I successfully broke the arrow and walked across the hot coals five times without even a smidge of a fire kiss (burnt bits) on either of my tootsies and felt absolutely ahhhhhhmazing!

This is it! Now's the time. There really has been no better time on this planet to go for it.

How magical can life be? What are the infinite possibilities?

I'll see you on the other side ☺ Wherever the other side may be.... ♥

Thanks for sharing this journey with me, big huge hugs and lotsa love,
Liz ♥

Postscript

When we moved to the countryside I kept affirming that everything I desire and require is right on my doorstep. On my list of things I would love to own, alongside my hopefully not too far in the distant future detached countryside cottage and retreat, are my very own hens and alpacas, a peacock, a yurt, a red phone box in our garden (I think they look so pretty restored) plus lots of other cool stuff.

In the village where we live (near enough on my doorstep) there's a fabulous peacock as well as a field at the bottom of our garden with Florence, Sonata and Psalm the Alpaca's and their feathery friends the hens who come and sit on our wall and provide us with delicious eggs. One of our neighbour's up the lane has put up a yurt in their front garden so I get to appreciate it every time I pass and we have a wonderfully restored red phone box at the end of our street with our names engraved in one of the panes of glass as we sponsored it! How totally magical is that! It's all so close in the here and now. That said, seeing I don't own these things I might change my affirmation to "everything I desire and require belongs to me and easily manifests in my life!"

Shall we affirm this together?

"Everything we desire and require belongs to us and easily manifests in our lives!"

Here's to EVEN MORE MAGIC flowing for us all....

How magical can we allow our lives to be?

If you would like to continue your journey of everyday magic, bring this book to life and connect with me and other like minded peeps directly each day, I have created a community ~ a tribe ~ where we can all share our experiences and co-create lots of magic together. It's called The Everyday Magic Community and you can learn lots more and join by visiting the following webpage on my blog ~
www.liz-green.com/everyday-magic-community/

Excited to connect with you all! ♥

Acknowledgements:

BIG HUGE THANK YOUS to each and every one of you for supporting me on this journey. ♥

Thank you to Cat Ian Greenwood aka my chap for your love and support over the last thirteen years we've spent together and more recently for putting up with my ongoing ramblings about the birth of this book.

Thanks to my mum and dad aka Maggie and Pete for bringing me into this world and teaching me all you know as well as supporting me every step of the way.

Thanks to all my friends, mentors for being there, I love you all dearly and appreciate your support during the good times and the not so good times too. You know who you are.

Thanks to the two Jackie's for helping me with my grammar and spelling and proofreading this book, it wouldn't have happened without you and how wonderfully synchronistic you both have the same names lol.

Thank you to the creative genius that is Corrine Lee-Cooke of Violet Lake Studio for creating such beautiful artwork for this cover and capturing the magic perfectly.

Thank you to everyone who had the faith and trust in me to complete this project and kindly donated to support this campaign, once again without this it may never have happened in the way it did.

From my heart to yours ❤
Thank you, thank you, thank you ❤